MYSTICISM
AND
SCIENCE

A Call for Reconciliation

Winchester, UK
Washington, USA)

First published by O Books, 2007
O Books is an imprint of John Hunt Publishing Ltd., The Bothy, Deershot Lodge, Park Lane,
Ropley, Hants, SO24 0BE, UK
office1@o-books.net
www.o-books.net

Distribution in:

UK and Europe
Orca Book Services
orders@orcabookservices.co.uk
Tel: 01202 665432 Fax: 01202 666219 Int. code (44)

USA and Canada
NBN
custserv@nbnbooks.com
Tel: 1 800 462 6420 Fax: 1 800 338 4550

Australia
Brumby Books
sales@brumbybooks.com
Tel: 61 3 9761 5535 Fax: 61 3 9761 7095

New Zealand
Peaceful Living
books@peaceful-living.co.nz
Tel: 64 7 57 18105 Fax: 64 7 57 18513

Singapore
STP
davidbuckland@tlp.com.sg
Tel: 65 6276 Fax: 65 6276 7119

South Africa
Alternative Books
altbook@peterhyde.co.za
Tel: 021 447 5300 Fax: 021 447 1430

Text copyright S. Abhayananda 2007

Design: Stuart Davies

ISBN-13: 978 1 84694 032 3
ISBN-10: 1 84694 032 X

A CIP catalogue record for this book is available from the British Library.

Printed in the US by Maple Vail

MYSTICISM AND SCIENCE

A Call for Reconciliation

by S. Abhayananda

BOOKS

Winchester, UK
Washington, USA

Dedicated to the memory of
Baba Muktananda
(1908-1982)

CONTENTS

ABOUT THE AUTHOR

The author of *Mysticism And Science* was born Stan Trout in Indianapolis, Indiana on August 14, 1938. After service in the Navy, he settled in northern California, where he pursued his studies in philosophy and literature. At the age of twenty-eight, he became acquainted with the possibility of mystical realization, and experienced a strong desire to realize God. Abandoning all other pursuits, he retired to a solitary life in a cabin hermitage in the mountain forests near Santa Cruz, California, where he devoted himself, for the next five years, to the realization of the Self. In the late Fall of 1966, he became enlightened by the grace of God, and realized his eternal Self. His life was dramatically changed from that moment on.

In 1971, he journeyed to India to live and study at the ashram of Swami Muktananda of Ganeshpuri; and in 1978 he was initiated by his master into the ancient Sarasvati Order of *sannyas*, and given the monastic name of Swami Abhayananda - a Sanskrit name, which means "the bliss of fearlessness." Since that time, Swami Abhayananda has taught the philosophy of Self realization and the art of meditation in a number of major cities throughout the U.S., and has lectured at numerous churches, colleges and universities. He presently resides on the Treasure Coast of Florida, where he continues to teach, write, and publish his works on the knowledge of the Self.

You are invited to learn more about his life and works at his website: www.swami-abhayananda.com.

PREFACE

One night, during a period of contemplation, I had a "mystical experience". I believe that this experience was a gift, not for me alone, but to be shared. And I have spent the past couple of decades attempting to share this very extraordinary knowledge that came to me through my mystical experience. However, it has long been evident to me that the public, and most especially the community of scientists who hold the key to the public trust, are not interested in hearing from me or my like as they continue to blunder along in their search for plausible conclusions about the reality in which we live. Mystics have never been taken seriously; some have been terribly persecuted and some even killed for their reportage of the knowledge they possess. Today, fortunately, we are only ignored. Still, this is a frustrating situation, because mystics want more than anything to share with others their knowledge and the joy which results from it. A mystic, one who has been given a glimpse into the true nature of God and the universe, may even feel that it is his God-given duty to share this knowledge for the greater benefit of all. But he has little likelihood of being heard in a materialistic and scientifically-oriented society such as ours.

Nonetheless, I am writing this book to offer my insights and those of other mystics for the purpose of providing the scientific community and those oriented toward a purely scientific worldview with some guidelines in their search for factual answers. What I have seen, as well as what other mystics have seen, has to my mind an unquestionable veracity; and so I feel that this vision, backed up by the corroborating experience of so many, is worthy of consideration and further investigation by the various representatives of science. I have no scientific training, so I apologize for any errors or wrong notions I may have put forward in this book that have exclusively to do with matters scientific.

What I am suggesting is not a proposal for replacing science with mysticism, but rather a cooperative partnership whereby science, following its own methods, makes use of the guidelines suggested by the expansive vision of the mystics. That vision is of a wholistic coordinated unfoldment of universal manifestation projected from and on the one invisible Intelligence. It is no doubt true that the rational comprehension of the source and ground of all existence brings with it a certain level of satisfaction in itself; but the inner revelation of identity with it brings a satisfaction that is unsurpassable, and seems to the recipient to be the summit of the entire evolutionary process. This great culmination of the desire for knowing can only be described by the mystic, but a reasoned explanation of the various mechanisms that are involved in the unfolding of this complex universe must be left to the scientist.

INTRODUCTION

A s is well known, Einstein worked on a "Unified Field Theory" during the latter part of his life without success. He was attempting to write a set of mathematical laws which would unify and explain in one theorem the nature of matter and the four scientifically known forces at work in the universe: the weak, electromagnetic, gravitational and strong forces that hold together all the observed matter in the universe. Since Einstein, the search for such a unifying theory has continued, so far without success. One of the most recent, called "Superstring Theory" or "The Theory of Everything" has been suggested as such a unifying theory.

The position put forth by the advocates of "Superstring Theory" claims to explain all these forces as well as all particles by suggesting an underlying "fundamental element" of both matter and forces in the shape of "strings" that are as small in relation to protons as a proton is to the Sun. These tiny strings are said to vibrate in such a way as to produce all the forces and particles of the physical realm, just as a violin string vibrates so as to produce all the different notes of the musical scale. However, not only are these supposed 'strings' much too small to ever be amenable to observation, but they require 10 or 24 dimensions, only four of which we are aware of today.

Scientists are agreed that, even if this "Theory of Everything" is indeed correct, it falls outside the realm of 'science' as it can never be proved by observation. It is merely a mathematical construct, a "metaphysical theory" on a par with all other metaphysical theories. And even if we were somehow able to conclude that it is correct, it still fails to address the origin of the existence of these strings, or to address the existence of the subjective reality, consciousness.

I intend to offer in this book a way to answer all the possible questions about the origin and manifestation of everything that exists, including consciousness. It is a vision that is backed by the experiential confirmation and the testimony of a notable few seers who have lived throughout the past several millennia. And though scientists have ignored it for all this time, it is a worldview that demands at least as fair and considered a hearing as that afforded to the Superstring theory. It requires, however, the acceptance of two complementary modes of knowledge: science and gnosis.

SCIENCE AND GNOSIS

Philosophers have long argued over just what constitutes "knowledge". Immanuel Kant (1724-1804), who is considered the final authority on epistemology, denied the possibility of the knowledge of ultimate reality. God, he said, is noumenal, and cannot therefore be understood by means of scientific knowledge, which relies on the confirmation of sense data regarding the phenomenal universe. This much is fine and true. He states further that God can only be understood through "moral faith"; i.e., belief based on speculative theory. He did not acknowledge or even consider that there might be a direct means of knowledge (gnosis), open only to mystical insight, that reveals the truth of God and the universal manifestation. But I would suggest that gnosis is not only a legitimate and valid means of knowledge, but a means which is necessary to complement and provide a conceptual framework for science.

Science obtains knowledge through deductive reasoning and through experimental evidence; i.e., the accumulation of sense data.

Gnosis obtains knowledge through direct perception in the state of identity with the Source. Gnosis does not consist of metaphysical speculation or doctrinaire expressions of religious faith; like science, it relies on direct perception, an experimental confirmation. Gnosis does not consist in a subject's perception of an object. It is a completely unique kind of knowledge in which the duality of subject and object is dissolved. It takes place in eternity, beyond all such opposites. Gnosis thus transcends all of the categories of knowledge postulated by Kant.

Gnosis is possible only when the subject and the object merge; it is the knowledge possessed by an individual when he or she transcends the activity of the limited ego, and becomes consciously merged in the Absolute, in God. Now, such knowledge is extremely rare; it is the province of the mystics. It is absolute knowledge which bestows absolute certainty. It goes without saying that science, in its search for demonstrable evidence relating to the cause or causes of the universe, has never yielded certainty; and, in principle, it never can. Only gnosis can bestow absolute certainty regarding the origin of the universe.

Yet there exists, and has existed for a long time, an intractable warfare between science and gnosis (mysticism), involving differences that appear on the surface to be irreconcilable. Each side in this war focuses singly on its own methodology of knowledge-gathering; each studies its own literature exclusively, and declares its own position to be based on experience. However, the experience of the scientist and the experience of the mystic are derived from different methodologies, different modes of knowledge. Science looks to reason and sense data, while the gnostic, or mystic, looks to interior contemplation. One is objective; the other is subjective. They each seek knowledge and certainty, but in dissimilar manners; the one by science, the other by gnosis.

Both of these words, *science* and *gnosis*, are of Greek origin, and mean "to know", but the knowledge is of two kinds. Each kind of knowledge has a long and well documented history: science has developed over the centuries through the positing of rational theories and the rigorous accumulation of physical data, modifying its position as reason, observation and data dictate; gnosis is also based on experience, but it is experience that is extra-sensual, supra-rational, and which comes only to a consciousness conforming to the gnostic method. Science is confirmed by evidence derived from empirical observation; gnosis is confirmed by evidence derived from introspective revelation.

Science, for example, has determined, through inspired theory, reason, and observation, that the universe of time and space began as a singularity referred to as "the big bang". Scientists have determined over the past century or so that at some point, about 15 billion years ago, an enormous amount of energy was released and expanded to create our universe. These scientists have even determined the temperatures and rate of acceleration of this energy in the first few seconds and minutes of its release, and have cataloged the material particles which were created as this energy cooled and solidified. They are also convinced that, prior to this "big bang", nothing else existed – not space, not time, not matter; but only this concentrated and unmanifested energy. They have further determined that approximately four and a half billion years ago remnants of an exploding star within this expanding universe, a supernova, condensed into our solar system; that sometime during the next few hundred million years, single-celled organisms bearing a molecule called DNA emerged on planet Earth; that these microbes then evolved, resulting in a prodigious display of living creatures, including *Homo sapiens*. It appears that our species, *homo sapiens*, emerged fairly recently, that is to say, in the last 150,000 years.

To this scientific theory mystics (gnostics) have no objection, as it is consistent with the knowledge obtained through gnosis. But it doesn't go far enough if we are interested in knowing the true beginning; i.e., where did this initial energy come from? Gnosis is able to provide the answer to this question. Science, however, is forever barred from providing such an answer, as science has limited itself by definition to empirically provable phenomena only. Gnostics have "seen" that the Source of all energy is noumenal. And since the Source of the energy which expanded to produce this universe is noumenal and not phenomenal, science is precluded by definition from its discovery. "Noumenon" is defined in Kantian terms as "a thing in itself, unable to be known through perception but postulated as the intelligible ground of a phenomenon." The intelligible ground is unknowable by science, but knowable by gnosis. Gnosis alone is capable of determining the reality of the noumenal from which all phenomena arise.

Gnosis results from the elimination of the ego-mechanism by which a person is limited to a separate individual identity. The ego-mechanism is a subtle mental obscuration that structures a false identification with the biological and psychological processes of individuation. Thus, instead of the real I-identity that is universal, one is limited to a false artificial identification with these isolated biological and psychological processes. The eternal Consciousness which is essentially one thereby becomes perceived in the awareness of the individual as a separate identity. This ego-mechanism may, however, under special introspective circumstances, be eliminated, immediately revealing to the human awareness the one eternal Consciousness, which is the real substratum of all individuated consciousnesses.

This experience of expanded awareness has occurred in numerous individuals throughout history. Some of the best known in the Western world are Jesus, the Buddha, Plotinus, Meister Eckhart and John of the Cross; but there are many more. They have described this experience of the one eternal Consciousness variously as "the union with God", "the extinction of the ego (*nirvana, samadhi*)", "enlightenment", "entering the kingdom of God", or the "mystic marriage of the soul and God." These experiences and their content are universal however, and are identical. The evidence for the occurrence of such a transcendence of the ego and the subsequent emergence into the awareness of and universal identity with the unitive and eternal Consciousness is overwhelming. It seems to me it is time for science to acknowledge the existence of such "revealed" knowledge, and to accord it the status of gnosis, while attempting to reconcile its own findings with the view of reality put forward by the gnostics.

More could be learned objectively about the obscurative and limiting ego-mechanism under which we all suffer, but its proper means of study, it seems to me, is subjective. The elimination of the obscurative and limiting effects of the ego-mechanism can only be accomplished by an introspective focus – whether by means of a dualistic devotional practice or by intense self-examination. Examples abound of representatives of both introspective methods who have obtained the ego transcending results.

But science, to its detriment, does not acknowledge this fact; indeed, science does not even acknowledge the possibility of gnosis.

Whatever is outside the purview of empirical science is regarded by its representatives as either nonexistent or simply unworthy of study. This is where the difficulty of reconciling science and gnosis begins. It is much like the position of some Middle Eastern countries who hold that reconciliation with the country of Israel cannot occur since they do not recognize the right of Israel to exist. If there is to be reconciliation between science and gnosis, gnosis must be acknowledged as a valid means of knowledge.

One has difficulty imagining that scientists will ever accept the declarations of mystics as science; and they needn't. But, as human beings interested in comprehending the whole of reality, they would do well to accept them as gnosis, as providing information through an alternate and complementary mode of knowledge that is essential along with science to a complete understanding of reality. The alternative is to remain forever locked in the mystery of a partially known and wholly incomprehensible universe.

Both of these two areas of knowledge, science and gnosis, must be acknowledged as valid means if we are to have a comprehensive overview of reality. As Albert Einstein once noted, "Science without religion [gnosis] is lame; religion without science is blind." This is more than merely a vague platitude; it is an insightful recognition that there are two distinct modes of knowledge, each of which, without the other, is incomplete, and both of which are required in order to comprehensively describe all aspects of the total reality.

The question then arises, "who speaks for gnosis?" or "what statements constitute true gnosis from among those statements by the many pretenders to gnosis?" And this is, perhaps, where the true difficulty lies. The answer is that it is the true mystics who speak for gnosis; it is the statements by those who have truly "seen" into the noumenal that constitute gnosis. And how do we separate out the true visionaries from the pretenders and from the many vastly diverse belief systems which presently circulate? Unfortunately, there is no easy or foolproof answer to that question. But, in gnosis as in science, there is a consensus among recognized authorities (mystics) on which we may rely. In my book, *History of Mysticism*, I have discussed the views of many such recognized mystics and shown that, despite the differences of language and culture, mystics throughout history have unanimously agreed on the elements of the noumenal reality.

For so many centuries science and gnosis have tread separate paths, scarcely acknowledging one another. And yet there must be an end to this isolationism. How long shall science pretend that the subtler mode of knowledge simply does not exist? In the past, religious faiths have often been in doctrinal opposition to the conclusions of science, and have had to adapt over time to the scientific view. The Copernican revolution, Galileo's observations, the Darwinian revelations, and many other scientific pronouncements, were resisted by the establishments of religious faith, and were many long years in being accepted and assimilated by them; but gnosis has never had a quarrel with science. It has simply not been acknowledged as existing apart from religious faith.

How can the revelations of Plotinus, Meister Eckhart, John of the Cross, and others in the Western mystical tradition simply be ignored? These few have been greatly multiplied by the addition to our knowledge of the lives and teachings of the great mystics of the Eastern traditions. Have they not all taught of the noumenal Source? And have they not, after their linguistic differences were accounted for, all presented identical truths?

These two camps, science and gnosis, have vied with one another over the centuries for the mind of the populace. And, for the past several centuries, science has been in the ascendancy in this war of ideals, and has dominated the attention of all of Western civilization. While I acknowledge the necessity of both of these two modes of knowledge, and have a deep love for science, I am a gnostic, not merely by conviction, but by experiential familiarity; and I wish, therefore, to present in this book a clarification of the knowledge obtained through gnosis as a guide to all those scientists and philosophers dedicated to the discovery of truth.

1

THE EXPERIENCE OF THE SELF

The basic elements of the Eastern world-view are also those of the world-view emerging from modern physics. ...Eastern thought–and, more generally, mystical thought–provides a consistent and relevant philosophical background to the theories of contemporary science; a conception of the world in which man's scientific discoveries can be in perfect harmony with his spiritual aims and religious beliefs. [1]

– Fritjof Capra

When Fritjof Capra's book, *The Tao of Physics*, was first published in 1975, many found the above statement an amazingly encouraging and promising insight. Conservative scientists, however, found it hogwash. The idea that mystical vision (gnosis) bore any resemblance to the findings of empirical scientific investigation, or that the two could in any way be reconciled was, to these scientists, a laughable proposition. I think that position needs to be reexamined. Science needs gnosis, and gnosis needs science.

Gnosis is generally regarded as belonging to the province of religion. But it is important to distinguish between religion and religious faith. "Religion" is a word derived from the Latin *religare*. *Ligare* means "to tie or bind"; its meaning is reflected in such derivatives as "ligament" and "ligature". *Religare* means to "re-tie, re-bind." It is interesting to note that the word, *yoga*, "to yoke", has a similar meaning. The word, "religion", therefore refers to "the re-uniting of the soul to God", the experience of the inner union which results in the knowledge that "I and the Father are one." Religious faith, on the other hand, is nothing more than a belief possessed by the mind that certain premises are true regarding God and His purposes. Religious faith may be possessed by anyone, but religion is something that is attained by only a few spiritually gifted souls. True "religion", therefore, is a spiritual revelation that comes only to those few who earnestly seek to be united with God; it is a gift of Grace. It may be called "enlightenment," "the mystic marriage," "the vision of God," or any number of other words or phrases. It is recognized by all religious faiths as a supernatural revelation of Truth that goes far beyond any and all doctrines or beliefs of religious faith.

Religious faiths are many; they are based for the most part on ideational interpretations of historical events. Religion is neither ideational nor historical; it is beyond both time and the vagaries of the mind. Religion, by definition, seeks only the union with God, the revelation of the Eternal. Religious faith seeks intellectual certainty and temporal satisfaction, and always falls short of both. Religion brings certainty of the Truth; religious faiths are fallible, each one contrary to another. See how the various religious faiths hold disparate views, each holding its own founders as well as its followers to be uniquely endowed with a cosmic and historical significance. The Jews regard themselves to be "the chosen of God"; Christians regard their founder to be "the Son of God," and themselves to be "saved" by that belief. Muslims regard Muhammed to be "the

Messenger of God," and his written words to be unerring and sacrosanct; Hindus regard Krishna to be an incarnation of God, and honor as sacred the rituals handed down in the Vedas; Buddhists worship the Buddha and his teachings as the preeminent and exclusive guide to enlightenment.

These are all examples of religious faith. Each is contrary to the other, and each regards its own followers as the only "true believers." However, among the followers of each of these religious faiths, there are a few who have known "religion"; i.e., who have known their identity with Divinity, having joined their souls to God. Such seers have existed and exist today among each of these religious faiths, attesting to a true "religion" that transcends as well as includes all religious faiths. Religion always fosters compassion, forbearance, and the recognition of the interconnected unity of all life. Religious faith is capable of promulgating absurdities; it is susceptible to ignorance and is capable of fostering activities directly contrary to the teachings of religion. In these recent days we have seen just how far afield such activities and absurdities can lead the followers of religious faith.

Scientists generally do not acknowledge that the noumenal Source of all manifestation is knowable; but there have been gnostics, myself among them, who have testified to their direct experiential knowledge of the noumenal, which they declare to be eternal. When the Eternal is revealed, they say, it is as though a tiny grain of sand had shed its "grain-ness", and become aware of its "sand-ness". "I am sand," such a grain might proclaim; "I cover all the shores of the world." Or, it is as though a tiny speck of foam, thrown up by a crashing wave, suddenly shed its identity with its tiny form and became aware "I am the vast ocean. I am the fathomless deep!"

When a man searches deeply enough within himself, his identity with a single form dissolves away, and he realizes, "I am all life; I am all that comprises this universe!" And then, focused intently upon this new vision, he sees even more deeply into himself, and he realizes that he is the formless and eternally living Consciousness which, while remaining unmoved and unchanged, continuously whole and unaltering, spews forth all this moving, changing panoply of universal form, as a man's mind creates a fantasy dream-world within itself.

Throughout history there have been a few who have declared that they have obtained mystical vision. Their testaments have been remarkably similar and explicit regarding the ultimate Source of the manifested universe. Among these few the most authoritative on the subject of cosmogony (the origin of the universe) are the authors of a number of Upanishads, the author of the Bhagavad Gita, Shankara, Plotinus, and Meister Eckhart; although there are many others who may be considered authoritative regarding other specific aspects of the mystical vision.

The mystic is gifted with a visionary experience that comes to him without his knowing how. His consciousness is elevated during a rare moment during contemplation to a noumenal level beyond his normal experience, and at once he is privy to an egoless state in which the transcendent reality becomes evident. There are a couple of levels to this mystical experience: at first he is aware of the absence of ownership of his body. The previous sense of an individual identity is gone, and he sees that his body is not the possession of an individuality, but belongs to the one current of existence which is universal, an ocean of energy in which all things and beings exist. He sees his body as a wave on that ocean, as a configuration of energy within a sea of energy, related to the universe as a pebble is to stone; as the mountains and valleys are to the earth.

He feels that, in being divested of an ego–that is, of an individual identity, he is now seeing himself and the world correctly; as though the veil of an illusory ego had been lifted, and now he is seeing truly and without the obfuscation of an erroneous orientation. He is like a scrap of wind in an infinite wind gale, like a wave on an infinite ocean, or like a golden trinket melted in a vat of gold. For a wave, the subsuming reality is the ocean; for a golden trinket, the subsuming reality is gold; for the individual consciousness, the subsuming reality is the one all-pervading Consciousness. No longer separate, his identity is merged into the larger substratum. If he entered this state from a state of prayer, there is no longer a deity, no longer an "I"; for, without the duality of "I" and "Thou", neither exists. He sees that former dualistic relationship as a product of the ego-mind's duality-producing habit. But now, all dualities are vanished. Not only is there no "I" or "Thou", there is no now or then, for time is also transcended in this state.

Dualities are judgments from an individual reference point, and without that egocentric reference point, dualities do not exist. Without the ego, there is only the timeless universal sea of existence, a vast ocean of conscious energy. Without the ego, where is love and hate? Where are peace and unrest, the heights and the depths, weeping and laughing? Without an ego, there is no life and death, no night or day, no music or silence, no motion or stillness. These all require a point of identity, and without that illusory perspective, there is only the one universal existence. When what *is* is the one energy doing everything, where is pride or regret? Furthermore, where is the distinction between body and soul? There is no division in this one conscious energy; it is homogeneous. There is only one. And this one existence is autonomous, independent, and wholly coordinated.

This is the first stage in the mystical experience. When the ego-sense falls away, one is aware only of the creative energy which manifests as the phenomenal universe and all its constituent parts. The mystic witnesses this revealed universal energy, not as a subject perceiving an object, a second; he perceives it as himself. It is I. And as he immerses himself more deeply into this awareness, a new clarity dawns as he reaches the second and ultimate stage of this introspective journey, and realizes: 'I am not just this creative flux; I am the Source of this creative power. I am the eternal Consciousness from which this outflow of energy comes.' This eternal Consciousness is primary to the creative energy, lying just above it, and is its Source. There is no higher. And It is known as one's true Self, the one transcendent Reality behind all universal manifestation.

That Self is Eternity. It is perfectly alone. It is perfect Consciousness and Bliss. There is nothing one can predicate of It. Yet, from that eternal Self a creative Energy fountains forth; from It time and space and the endless universe pours forth and returns in the same manner as breath flows out and returns in the case of a human being. It is a cyclic ebbing and flowing of the creative energy of the One which bursts into being like an exhaled breath, expanding and spreading, only to be reversed as in an inhalation, extinguishing what had been produced. The mystic experiences this as occurring from himself, since he is united, at one, with the one Self.

My own mystical experience came suddenly, and opened to me the initial awareness that I, my bodily self, was integral to the universal ocean of energy which is this cosmos. (For a description of the circumstances leading to this experience, please see my book, *The Supreme Self.*) I was not a separate being in the world, but a wave on that ocean of God's activity, and belonged to Him (the one Existence) and existed in Him. My sense of an individual identity (the ego) had vanished, and I was seeing my existence from the true perspective of one without a separate and distinct vantage point amidst the vast creative flux. As my vision expanded, I became aware of my deeper identity as the unmanifest Source of all manifestation, the one Consciousness, the sole Origin of all being. Whatever separate identity I entered that experience with had become transparent, and vanished in the dawning awareness of myself as the eternal Consciousness Itself. I knew my true identity as the original One from whom all is derived; I was the unchanging and eternal Consciousness. Yet I was also aware of the cyclical outflow from Me of the universal array, in a motion similar to the exhalation and inhalation of a breath. From the vantage of Eternity, it seemed that the creation and dissolution of the universe took place in the space of a leisurely breath. And its expansion and contraction could be seen in its entirety, as one might watch a balloon repeatedly expand and contract as one breathed into it.

Reflecting on this experience, it was clear that while the Eternal, the transcendent Absolute, which we will hereafter refer to as "God", is, in Himself, beyond all activity, His Creative Power produces a universe of form and activity. The Creative Power of God (called in other traditions *Nous, Logos, Prakriti, Maya, Shakti*) is not different from God. It is His Power of creation, and is in no way separate from Him. While He remains entirely alone in His transcendent purity and unchangeability, He projects the cosmic drama by His own inherent

Power.

When we try to imagine such a dual state of being, we cannot, because, for us, such a paradoxical state cannot exist. But, for the absolute Ground, or "God", such a paradoxical condition exists. In Himself, He is empty of thought or activity, pure Consciousness unmarred; and yet, He effortlessly "projects", or "emanates" an "Energy" which transforms itself into an inconceivably complex universal drama in which stars explode, civilizations rise and fall, and human beings evolve to know within themselves the Source and Creator. And then, the entire expanding cosmos reverses its expansion and is drawn back into its unmanifested state, once again residing as pure potential in the pure Energy of the Creative Power of God. This cycle of creation/dissolution repeats itself endlessly. Yet, throughout this cosmic evolution and involution, He remains One, eternal, in His own Bliss.

While I have seen most clearly that the universe is "breathed out" by the great Consciousness, I have not seen into the particulars of it, but have seen only the wholeness of it from the perspective of Eternity. In that vision, the expansion and contraction of the universe occurs in the space of a breath. All those billions of earth-years required for the genesis, expansion, and subsequent reabsorption of the universe are crammed into an eternal overview which does not observe the tiny interactions of small particles, but rather sees the entirety only as a momentary universal expansion and contraction. Individual lives are not seen; the rising and falling of civilizations is not seen; the nativity and death of stars is not seen. From the vantage point of Eternity, it is like watching the spraying out of a breath, and its subsequent withdrawal. The details of its enactment are not seen, but only its occurrence.

So, clearly, I cannot explain in anything remotely similar to scientific language the details of that appearance and disappearance of the universe. Its Source is, of course, the one eternal Consciousness (which we call "God"). He is eternal (He does not live in Eternity; He *is* Eternity), which means He is beyond time and space; and yet, He produces a universe of time and space, which, though it is not Himself, is a product of Himself, as our own breath is a product of each of us. It is a universe produced from Himself, since there is nothing else besides that One from which it could be composed. This universe, of which we are a part, appears to us as substance, but, as science has shown, it is a tenuous substance at best, made as it is of dream-stuff, or, more accurately, of God-stuff. It is produced from the one Eternal, unmanifest, absolute Consciousness, and has but a transitory existence. After it is reabsorbed back into the Eternal, it is sent forth once again in what is apparently an interminably repeated cycle of becoming and dis-becoming, expanding and contracting.

Also, I was not privy to the so-called "subtle" realms of spirit; I saw nothing there of angels, spirit-guides, or souls. This does not imply that these do not exist at the phenomenal level, however. My vision was one of identity with the Eternal, my original transcendent Source and ultimate being. I was able to see also, as mentioned above, the outflow and influx of the universal cosmos, but nothing of its manner of evolution. Some others may have direct knowledge of the subtle realms proceeding from the Creative Power of God, which in turn produces the material universe; but I do not.

I wish very much that I could provide some insight into the process of this activity, but I cannot. His secret method will have, for the time being, to remain His secret. I can shed no light on the transformation from God-energy to formative "matter", and so I am unable to definitively deflate the pride of the present-day physicists, with their hadrons and leptons and quarks of many colors. Suffice it to say that, ultimately, all must be traced back to Him. Is it His play? His compulsion? His involuntary reflex? I cannot shed any light on His motivation or his purpose; except to say it seemed to me to be an expansion of His love or joy. I only know that I am His appearance, made of His light, and, for one brief space of time/eternity, He revealed Himself to me, and made me know that my existence is His existence. That is all I know, and probably all I need to know.

The following is an observation of that eternal Self, written during the direct experience of it:

SONG OF THE SELF

O my God, even this body is Thine own!
Though I call to Thee and seek Thee amidst chaos,
Even I who seemed an unclean pitcher amidst Thy waters –
Even I am Thine own.
Does a wave cease to be of the ocean?
Do the mountains and the gulfs cease to be of the earth?
Or does a pebble cease to be stone?
How can I escape Thee?
Thou art even That which thinks of escape!

Even now, I speak the word, "Thou", and create duality;
I love, and create hatred;
I am in peace, and am fashioning chaos;

Standing on the peak, I necessitate the depths.

But now, weeping and laughing are gone;

Night is become day;

Music and silence are heard as one;

My ears are all the universe.

All motion has ceased; everything continues.

Life and death no longer stand apart.

No I, no Thou; no now, or then.

Unless I move, there is no stillness.

Nothing to lament, nothing to vanquish,

Nothing to pride oneself on;

All is accomplished in an instant.

All may now be told without effort.

Where is there a question?

Where is the temple?

Which the Imperishable, which the abode?

I am the pulse of the turtle;

I am the clanging bells of joy.

I bring the dust of blindness;

I am the fire of song.

I am in the clouds and in the gritty soil;

In pools of clear water my image is found.

I am the dust on the feet of the wretched,

The toothless beggars of every land.

I have given sweets that decay to those that crave them;

I have given my wealth unto the poor and lonely.

My hands are open – nothing is concealed.

All things move together of one accord;

Assent is given throughout the universe to every falling grain.

The Sun stirs the waters of my heart,

And the vapor of my love flies to the four corners of the world;

The moon stills me, and the cold darkness is my bed.

I have but breathed, and everything is rearranged

And set in order once again.

A million worlds begin and end in every breath, And in this breathing, all things are sustained.

2

ON LEARNED IGNORANCE

I do not understand how the scientific approach alone, as separated from a religious approach, can explain an origin of all things. It is true that physicists hope to look behind the 'big bang' and possibly to explain the origin of our universe as, for example, a type of fluctuation. But then, of what is it a fluctuation and how did this in turn begin to exist? In my view, the question of origin seems always left unanswered if we explore from a scientific view alone. [2]

–Charles Townes

The above quote by a respected scientist reveals the present quandary of science. Scientists are able to go so far, but no further, due to the inherent limitations of the scientific method, which disallows the inclusion of undemonstrable suppositions. Many scientists of today feel that, either they have reached the limits of empirical knowledge, or are fast approaching that end. 'There is so much we simply do not know and probably shall never be able to know', they complain. Consider, I would suggest, broadening the definition of knowledge to include gnosis; and borrow from that branch of knowledge the insights gained by the great mystics. Take the larger truths revealed to them regarding the origin of energy and consciousness as premises on which to build, and incorporate those premises into your search for demonstrable evidence.

It should be evident that the scientist and the mystic are very similar in their motivations. Both seek to know the truth. But whereas the scientist, relying upon his perceptions in the relative world, is only able to discover relative truths, the mystic discovers the absolute truth to which the scientist, with his enormous intellectual knowledge, may never find entry. Scientists find it almost impossible to accept the premise of God as the originator of the universe; they find it impossible to accept an ultimate Cause which they can't intellectually comprehend, and so they ignore the experiential evidence of gnosis. I think too that many scientists confuse religion with religious faith—particularly, the Judaeo-Christian faith with which many of them are most familiar. Many simply go on searching throughout their careers for an empirically substantiated cause until their brains waste away and they then realize, perhaps on their deathbeds, that the reality of God must be accepted, even though they cannot comprehend Him or substantiate His existence empirically.

My admiration for the scientific method and for scientists in general is great. The results of their inherent desire to discover the nature of this world have brought us not only great insights into the nature of our world, but also innumerable instances of practical knowledge, material welfare and comfort, and they are due our praise and gratitude. But the scientific method cannot reveal the transcendent Cause of phenomena. Reason cannot discover It; It is revealed only in the contemplative state, beyond the intellect, beyond the imagination, by what can only be termed God's grace. All efforts to frame an intellectual defense of God's existence have failed to be efficacious. It is beyond proving, except by direct vision.

Those of us who have "seen" God have declared that vision, but little attention has been paid to these declarations. Great visionaries like Jesus, Plotinus, Philo Judaeus, Meister Eckhart, Ramakrishna, and others have told of their direct apperception of God, but even these first-hand accounts are rejected by those of a 'scientific' turn of mind. I am adding my own testament to these others, but it is unlikely that many will listen.

Nicholas of Cusa, a fifteenth century Cardinal of the Church, who was also a mystic, wrote a book called, *De docta ignorantia*, "On Learned Ignorance". In it, and in his other writings, he made clear to the dialecticians of his time that no amount of reasoning, no amount of intellectual effort, could reveal That which was beyond the reach of words and intellectual conceptions. He pointed out to them that when they reached that understanding which allowed them to acknowledge that all their learning had only brought them, and could only bring them, to know that they did not know, then they will have reached that state of "learned ignorance" wherefrom they could truly begin to embark on their spiritual journey of introspection to true knowledge. "Reason," said Nicholas,

Strives for knowledge and yet this natural striving is not adequate to the knowledge of the Essence of God, but only to the knowledge that God ... is beyond all conception and knowledge. [3]

... That wisdom (which all men by their very nature desire to know and consequently seek after with such great affection of mind) is known in no other way than that it is higher than all knowledge and utterly unknowable and unspeakable in all language. It is unintelligible to all understanding, immeasurable by all measure, improportionable by every proportion, incomparable by all comparison,... unimaginable by all imagination, ... and because in all speech it is inexpressible, there can be no limit to the means of expressing it, being incognitable in all cognition ... 4

The rational intellect cannot discover the truth of God. It can only throw up objections to the idea of such an incomprehensible being. From a purely intellectual standpoint, the idea of an absolute Source of all existence is replete with rational objections. Here, for example, from a recent book by a respected scientist, are three 'paradoxes of cosmogony' which are listed as rational scientific objections to the possibility of such an Origin:

Number one is *"There can be no effect without a cause. Whatever events transpired near the outset of time, each must have been caused by some prior event. So we can never attain an account of the very beginning."*

It is true that there must be a cause to every effect. But the one absolute Consciousness, which we call God, is not an effect of anything. It is unique in that It is eternal and uncaused. And while It is unmanifested and indescribable, it contains within It a creative power to manifest form. The human consciousness, though empty of thought forms in its pure state, also has a power to manifest thoughts, words and dreams which previously had no existence. It is in a similar manner that the one eternal Consciousness manifests a universe of worlds. It cannot be comprehended intellectually, but it can be seen in the depths of one's soul. I have seen this production from the eternal Consciousness much more clearly than I see these words before me.

It should be stated that if the ultimate origin of the universe were of a phenomenal nature, science would eventually be able to discover it. If it is not; in other words, if it is of a noumenal nature (as it is), science would never be able to discover it. There was a period during which science – in particular, particle physics – sought to discover the secret of matter by smashing it to bits, and hoping to find the ultimate answer to what matter is made of. Instead, all they discovered were more and more bits. The outskirts of science are the borders of phenomenality; science is bound by its own definition to go no further. It should be clear that the long history of science tells the story of the failed search for an "originating principle", while the long history of gnosis tells the story of the many who have known that originating principle, and declared it time and time again.

The second paradox is, *"You can't get something from – or for – nothing. The 'origin' of the universe, if that concept is to have any meaning, must create the universe out of nothing. Therefore there can be no logical explanation of genesis."*

The absolute Consciousness that is God does not create a universe out of nothing. He creates it out of Himself. As the human consciousness contains within it a latent plethora of potential thoughts, words, and dreams, in a similar manner the one eternal Consciousness emanates from Himself a universe of worlds. When it is seen in the mystical vision, it is most wonderful and awe-inspiring; and, while it is alogical, it is not illogical.

The third paradox is, *"Regardless of its net energy, the universe must have originated from another system, and that system must in turn have had an origin of some sort. And so we are caught in infinite regress."* [5]

I cannot say definitely that God was not produced from some previous God; I have no way of knowing that. Yet it seems unlikely; for what can precede eternity? There is no 'before' or 'after' there.

Certainly, as far as this universe is concerned, He is the end of the line. To be united with God is to be gifted with absolute certainty regarding the Source and nature of existence. When all has been reduced to one, there is no further reduction. There is no further question when you have come to the origin of existence itself. Where would you regress to?

Many make much of the question in some circles whether this universe, and particularly humanity, came into existence through creation and intelligent design or through the development of natural evolution. The fact is, both are true. Religion is not in conflict with science on this issue; it is only religious faith, relying upon the literal interpretation of ancient sectarian texts that is in conflict with science. Darwin, who brought to light the concept of the evolution of species, saw only the physical manifestations of the evolution of life forms, but religion (gnosis) confirms that evolution is "built-into" the fabric of the universe. It is the underlying principle of creation, evident in the stars, planets, and all life forms. There is a progressive unfoldment that takes place within the space-time universe of creative energy. But this in no way contradicts the fact that the entirety was initiated by and from the Creator.

Creationism and evolution do not contradict one another, and any supposition that they are somehow opposed to one another represents a failure to see the larger picture. The instigation of the 'big bang' and its evolving results, constituting the universe – the formation of galaxies, the emergence of life, consummating in man and his eventual development into a god-like state – is all contained in the Creator's act. The evolution that is evidenced in the universe is an evolution of intelligent design and no accident of fortuitous circumstances. It is God's unfoldment of Himself upon His own screen in a deliberate manner; and though we are as yet incapable of discerning its purpose and end, all will no doubt be made clear in the end.

It is my contention that the picture of reality described by the gnostics may serve usefully as a hypothetical basis for scientific investigation. What, for example, would we expect to find in the phenomenal universe if the Source and Origin of the universe is indeed an eternal Consciousness endowed with a creative Power (Energy)? Could we expect that a projection of that conscious energy might erupt into a space/time explosion, thrusting energy outward to quickly become particulate matter? And could we possibly expect to see life and conscious beings emerge from that primordial matter in the course of an evolutionary progression? More specifically, how would the world and its creatures behave if it and they consisted of such an expanded conscious energy? Is it possible that those conscious beings, outcroppings and extensions of that originating Consciousness/Energy, would be able to eventually intuit within themselves a guiding intelligence, and, under extreme circumstances, to return in consciousness to their Origin and perceive their original (and eternally present) Identity? Since these proposed effects do indeed exist in the phenomenal world, is not the premise, i.e., the nature of the original cause as described by the mystics, therefore not only possible but probable? Certainly, it is much more probable than the notion that a "singularity", an infinitely dense pocket of heated energy, just showed up in the void out of nowhere, exploded, and produced time, space, matter, life and conscious beings with no intelligible source.

PRAISE GOD

I'm here to sing the praise of God, and so I shall.
And let none think belief's the basis of my song,
Or words I've read in high-flown works;
The subject of my song is what I've seen,
What He's revealed to my most meager sight
In holy quiet night's retreat.

Though many have praised His creation –
Its beauties, and its grandeur;
I would praise Him in His unborn formless Essence
Where He lives unmoved, and happily serene.

Though He breathes forth the immense and tumultuous cosmos,
Enjoying the drama of its unfolding activity,
He remains clearly indivisible
And perfectly unmoved within Himself,
Continually aware that He alone exists.
There is no other; so all's contained in Him.

Serene, yet keenly awake, He spreads
His outflowing radiance in every direction;
Delight, unbounded and uninterrupted,
Permeates Him and all He proffers.
In one breath, He flashes forth the universal array,
And then withdraws it all again,
Only to breathe once more and fling the stars
And galaxies wheeling on their rounds again.
For creatures, it's an almost endless parade

Of eon upon eon, unfathomably deep in time's recess;
But for him, who knows no change or movement,
It's but a moment's breath.
And yet the greatest wonder is that every soul breathed forth
Is but a time-wrought image of Himself;
And each one, being His by virtue of its life in Him,
Is capable of finding at its core that One who fashioned it to life.

As a figure in a dream awakes to know he is the dreamer,
Each soul, when it awakes, discovers it is none but Him.
He appears as though in a house of many mirrors,
Fragmented into a million images, yet all are Him;
It's but a masquerade.

And when the soul awakes to know its deathless Self,
Beyond imagined dreams of personhood,
It knows that forever it has lived serene and blissful,
Just beyond the dream.

It learns that all the devilish battles and tortuous travails
Were but a thought-parade in which, for the briefest time
It marched, all unawares, to finally break away
And find its way to freedom from time's tumultuous play.

To find such freedom one must look within,
And, gaining clarity of mind, discover who one really is.
Who one really is is Him! For none exists but Him alone.
It's true! He lives alone in high eternity;
But He lives as well as you and me.

It's you and me who lives in that eternal sky
While playing out our destined roles below.
Two selves, one vigilant while tossing out the stars,
The other strutting on this stage of dreams,
Oblivious to the other, her only Self and Source.

The all-encompassing, all-sustaining Self of all
Is quite alone, and quite contained
Without a drama to behold,
Until He beams Himself in outward radiance
As particles and galaxies and separate living things
In bright array,
To people all these worlds with beings
Conscious of their knowing selves.
His game: to lead them all within themselves
In stage by stage to knowledge of the ways of things,
And finally to awareness of that deeper Self
Who flung them forth to journey home
To know the ultimate Truth that they are Him.
Awaking to that joyful knowledge,
The spell of separation falls away
Along with fear and worry, woes and cares.
And, lifted up in mind and spirit,
The knower lives in peace and joy beyond this world
Alone, eternal, as all in all.
He knows the universal design to be his own;
He walks in freedom. His soul is blest.
Praise God!

3

THE UNCERTAIN SCIENCE

The principle of causality must be held to extend even to the highest achievements of the human soul. We must admit that the mind of each one of our great geniuses— Aristotle, Kant, or Leonardo, Goethe or Beethoven, Dante or Shakespeare—even at the moment of its highest flights of thought or in the most profound inner workings of his soul—was subject to the causal fiat and was an instrument in the hands of an almighty law which governs the world. [6]

– Max Planck

There was a revolution in science during the last century called "Quantum Theory" which challenged the notions of certainty and causality in the world of microphysics. It all began in 1927 with an article entitled, "On The Intuitive Content Of Kinematics and On The Mechanics of Quanta", in which the Principle of Indeterminacy was first expounded by physicist Werner Heisenberg.

Heisenberg discovered the Principle of Indeterminacy (or Uncertainty) by a process of mathematics called "matrix mechanics" which, in effect, proved the practical impossibility of simultaneously determining both the position and momentum of an electron. The mathematical proof can be approximately demonstrated by the following illustration: Suppose you wished to illumine an electron with a photon of light in order to determine its position. You would find that each time you did, you drastically altered the position of the electron by that very photon of light. This is because to see something as small as an electron, one must use light of a very small wave-length, which is at the same time of a very high frequency; i.e., high energy. So, by pin-pointing its position, you would inadvertently knock it helter-skelter, and hence lose certainty of its momentum; conversely, if you used light of a longer wave-length, i.e., not so intense, you would get an idea of the momentum of the electron, but you would not have enough clarity to get an accurate 'fix' on its position. Or, if you tried another method, of narrowing the lens of the microscope, thus requiring less light, you would have a better idea of the path of the electron, but because light waves bend, or diffract, more as the aperture of the lens is narrowed, the distortion would cause the position to be obscured.

So, what Heisenberg discovered was that, because of the very nature of matter and of light, the more clearly one was able to determine an electron's position, the more obscure became its momentum (velocity times mass). And the more one focused on the momentum, the less information one could get about its exact position. In other words, no matter how carefully one attempted to measure the position and momentum of a particle, there would always be some uncertainty in the measurement. This is 'The Principle of Uncertainty'.

It became evident that one simply could not determine the causes of microphysical events, as the ability to perceive the factors necessary to such a determination was precluded by the very nature of light and matter. For that reason, a group of physicists led by Neils

Bohr renounced the attempt to describe the exact behavior of individual particles, and began studying the probable events in the sub-atomic world by means of calculating probabilities. By this method, they were not able to predict individual events, but could give the calculated probability for the occurrence of one possibility or another.

This was all very good, and very useful—so far as it went. But then this group of physicists decided that since they could not observe and measure individual causal factors, then those individual causal factors did not exist! Bohr wrote:

> It was necessary to give up describing the behavior of individual atoms in space and time according to the principle of causality and to imagine that nature could make amongst various possibilities a free choice which was not governed by any considerations other than probability. [7]

According to this new brand of physics, any given subatomic particle behaves as it does without any relationship to any event preceding it in a causal chain: causality is not observed; therefore, causality does not exist. This opinion, held by Bohr and Heisenberg who were based in Denmark, came to be known as the 'Copenhagen Interpretation' of quantum mechanics, and was widely accepted by physicists around the world as the only proper scientific approach to quantum phenomena. Physicists, no longer able to describe the trajectories of quantum particles in space—because of the Uncertainty principle—described quantum states in terms of an equation devised by physicist Erwin Schrödinger, which he called the "wave-function". This wave-function could only describe the probable location of a quantum particle; its actual position remained ambiguous until the "collapse" of the wave-function, by which is meant the collapse of all possibilities into a single outcome based on actual measurement or direct observation.

Thus, quanta were suspended in a realm of non-existence—neither here nor there—until they were actually observed by a subject. Until the wave-function "collapsed", one was not only unable to predict a particle's location, but the particle's location could not be said to exist. Naturally, this methodology, while providing accurate results, led to some bizarre conclusions. Consider the paradox of "Schrödinger's cat, a thought-experiment in which a cat is sealed into a box with a Geiger counter connected to a hammer, along with a vial of cyanide. A radioactive nucleus is then introduced into the box which has a fifty-fifty chance of disintegrating in the next half hour. If it does, it will register on the Geiger counter, which will in turn set off the release of the hammer and break the vial of cyanide, thus killing the cat. If the radioactive particle does not disintegrate in that time, the cat will live.

The paradox involves the question, 'If the lid of the box is not yet lifted to observe the cat after a half-hour, is the cat alive or dead? According to the laws governing the use of the wave-function, the cat is neither dead nor alive. Neither possibility has any "real" status; that has to await the actual lifting of the box's lid; i.e., the collapse of the wave-function. Up until that time the cat is neither alive nor dead. But this is clearly counterintuitive. One is willing to suspend the reality of a particle's location in a nebulous realm of possibility, but a cat, we must believe, is either alive or dead, regardless of its observation. This was the untenable position into which quantum physics had relegated itself.

Quantum physics, practiced according to the Copenhagen interpretation, had abandoned the strict causality of classical physics in
favor of the determination of probabilities, and held that until actually observed, quantum states had no quantifiable reality.
Unfortunately, this view cannot be contradicted by empirical evidence, for it is no doubt true that causal relationships on the subatomic level are indeterminable by observation, as explained by
Heisenberg's Principle; but it is just as undoubtedly true that such
causal relationships are not proven to be non-existent. To borrow a
phrase, "absence of evidence is not evidence of absence." Not all
physicists, however, accepted these new ideas that quanta had no
"real" existence, but only a probable one, and that causality had to
be abandoned. Einstein, along with a few others, protested the aban-
donment of causality: "God is sophisticated," he said; "but He is not
malicious."

Einstein argued that although quantum mechanics, utilizing the
method of calculating probability, is successful in dealing with the
problems of microphysics, it is not a complete theory accounting for
every element of reality, but is merely a stopgap measure to provide
information in the absence of our ability to see the invisible progression of causes, or "hidden variables", which underlie apparently
causeless microphysical phenomena. He continued to argue against
the 'Copenhagen Interpretation' of quantum mechanics till the end
of his life, often reasserting his belief that "God does not play with
dice." Nonetheless, most physicists believed that even if those "hidden variables" or invisible causal progressions existed, they could
never be demonstrated or calculated; therefore, it was pointless to
regard them as relevant or meaningful to scientific endeavor. This
position was very well summed by physicist Banesh Hoffman, in his

book, *The Strange Story Of The Quanta*:

> As for the idea of strict causality, not only does science, after all these years, suddenly find it an unnecessary concept, it even demonstrates that according to the quantum theory strict causality is fundamentally and intrinsically undemonstrable. *Therefore, strict causality is no longer a legitimate scientific concept*, and must be cast out from the official domain of present-day science. [my italics.] [8]

Let us follow very closely the logic implied in the above statement: (a) a legitimate scientific concept is one which is demonstrable by physical evidence; (b) at the subatomic level, causality has been shown to be undemonstrable; (c) therefore, causality is not a legitimate scientific concept.

Here, we see clearly stated the inherent limitations of empirical science, revealing its inability to account for all aspects of experiential reality. This is not intended as a criticism of science; it is merely an acknowledgement of the oft-recognized and understood principle that science does not extend to the undemonstrable. By its own definition, it excludes itself from the realm of metaphysics; that is to say, from the postulation of undemonstrable causes. And, since Heisenberg has shown the impossibility of determining or demonstrating the causes of subatomic events, then clearly, the postulation of such causes cannot be a "legitimate scientific concept" and must be cast out of its domain.

Nevertheless, we must see that it is equally beyond the province of empirical science to imply, as Bohr and his followers have done, that because it is undemonstrable, causality at the microphysical level does not exist. For, while it is certain that science must dismiss causality from its concern, it does not mean that causality does not exist, or that it is beyond knowing. It is only by virtue of the conceit that knowledge—and truth itself—is limited to the domain of 'science' that one can uphold such nonsense.

Let us understand this issue clearly; it is important to distinguish between science and gnosis, and to understand the capabilities and limitations of each: empirical science is incapable of demonstrating causes; its only business is and has always been simply to describe the behavior patterns of phenomena. For though science is capable of describing the phenomena of motion, inertia, gravity, mass, space, energy, etc., it has never been able to determine the cause of these phenomena, as science is precluded in principle from the realm of the invisible, undemonstrable source of all phenomena, the Cause of the manifestation of phenomena. For the determination of the Cause, science must defer to the seers, the mystics. The role of science is then to show whether or not the statements of the seers are consistent with demonstrable evidence.

The knowledge of the mystics, which we designate as gnosis, is subjective and undemonstrable, but it is knowledge nonetheless, confirmed through experience by countless other mystics. Gnosis is not simply a designation for any and every kind of subjective knowledge; it refers only to the form-transcending knowledge of universal Identity, the direct knowledge of the Absolute, the Godhead. Historically, this knowledge has been relegated to the category of religion, and equated with belief; yet it is, and should be re-established as, the summit of human knowledge, and the guiding light for science.

Science and gnosis do not contradict each other; they are complementary means of knowledge appropriate to a reality which consists of two contrary but complementary aspects. Gnosis looks to the realm of Consciousness, while science looks to the realm of empirical phenomena; yet both, as complementary viewpoints, are absolutely necessary to the whole and complete knowledge of reality. Indeed, it is the omission of either one of these complementary viewpoints that so often gives rise to misunderstanding and error.

WHEN YOU SING THE NAME OF GOD IN YOUR HEART

When you sing the name of God in your heart,
When you sing the name of God in your heart,
The curtains of your soul then part
And the truth comes streaming in.

When you sing the name of God in your heart,
A new awareness dawns,
And the voice that called is silenced
In the silence that is Him.

Who calls? Whose awareness sings of God?
Who stands behind the calling and the song?
The very breath that sings His name
Is He whose name is called.

The caller recognizes suddenly from whence the song arose
And turns his attention to the "I" from whom all "I"s derive.
The consciousness that seeks His embrace

Is conscious of itself, above the breathing, beneath the song,
And finds, amazed, the One it sought.

How delicate the thread that holds this knowledge close!
Awareness held aloft upon its very Self!
No call, no song; but only flawless clarity of mind
Above the clamor of the song and breath,
Above the sense of self.
This eternal breathless sky of Mind
Is the Source of breath and song;
The seeker and the One who's sought
Reveal that they are one.

4

THE IMPLICATE ORDER

Relativity and, even more important, quantum mechanics have strongly suggested (though not proved) that the world cannot be analyzed into separate and independently existing parts. Moreover, each part somehow involves all the others: contains them or enfolds them....This fact suggests that the sphere of ordinary material life and the sphere of mystical experience have a certain shared order and that this will allow a fruitful relationship between them.[9]

–David Bohm

According to the mystics who have seen into the nature of reality at the noumenal level, God, the one absolute Consciousness, is the Source and Cause of all phenomena, manifesting the universe by His creative Power in a manner similar to the projection of thought in the mind of an individual. This Divine Thought contains implicit within it the conscious Intelligence of the Source; and implicit in it also is the entire design and evolution of the universe, from its initial coming into being to all the refinements and transformations necessary in the process of its ultimate realization. Science does not recognize such a scenario as tenable, and relegates the visionary knowledge of the mystics to the category of speculative metaphysics. However, one brave scientist stepped forward to acknowledge the possibility that the mystic's vision could provide a basis for a true and consistent worldview; his name is

David Bohm.

David Bohm (1917-1992) was born in Wilkes-Barre, Pennsylvania on December 20, 1917. His father was a Jewish furniture dealer, but David went to college, receiving his B.Sc. degree from Pennsylvania State College in 1939 and his Ph.D. in physics at the University of California, Berkeley, in 1943. At U.C. Berkeley, he studied with Robert Oppenheimer; and when Oppenheimer went to Los Alamos to work on the "Manhattan Project", he remained as research physicist. He remained at Berkeley, working on the Theory of Plasma and on the Theory of Synchroton and Syndrocyclotrons until 1947, when he took a position as an Assistant Professor at Princeton University, working on Plasmas, Theory of Metals, Quantum Mechanics and Elementary Particles. It was there he met and had regular meetings with Albert Einstein.

In 1949, during the repressive McCarthy era, Bohm was called before the House Un-American Activities Committee, and asked to testify against Robert Oppenheimer who was being accused of Communist sympathies. Bohm refused to testify, and was thereafter tried and acquitted. But the damage had been done; he was fired from his position at Princeton, and was unable to find work in this country. He then moved to Brazil where he taught briefly at the University of Sao Paolo. He also taught for a brief time in Israel before moving to Bristol, England in 1957. In 1961, he became professor of physics at Birkbeck College of the University of London, and remained there for the next 30 years, writing and publishing his several books: *Causality and Chance in Modern Physics* (1957), *The Special Theory of Relativity* (1966), *Wholeness and the Implicate Order* (1980), and *Science, Order and Creativity* (1987). David Bohm died in 1992.

In the 1950's David Bohm was widely considered one of the most talented and promising physicists of his generation. But his primary work from the 1950's to the 1990's—the ongoing development of his "causal interpretation" (which he later referred to as an "ontological interpretation") of quantum mechanics as an alternative to the standard 'Copenhagen Interpretation'—was met with dismissive hostility by the majority of the world physics community. In an attempt to provide a scientific formulation of quantum physics consistent with the mystic's vision of a Divine origin and manifestation of our world, Bohm had presented a theory called 'The Implicate/Explicate Order', in which he formulated in scientific language the postulation of the "unfoldment" of the order of the phenomenal world from an "enfolded" order in a noumenal Source, referring to these two as "the implicate order" and "the explicate order".

According to his theory, the implicate order is an invisible substratum containing the archetypal template for the emergence and dynamics of both matter and consciousness, much the way the mind is the archetypal template of conscious thoughts produced from it. And in his wonderfully lucid writings he endeavored to explain how an "explicate order" such as this perceived universe is has its source in and unfolds from this implicate, or enfolded order. The implicate order implicitly contains the explicate order, and the explicate order explicitly contains the implicate order.

Bohm theorizes that, in the implicate order, all things, including particles, are interconnected in a way that transcends space and time. This is because the implicate order is an integral noumenal substratum resembling a transcendent Thought-matrix which generates, forms, and organizes the constituents of the explicate order. Quanta appear wavelike (as does thought) until they are observed; that is, witnessed by a conscious observer. Then they become particles; i.e., individualized 'things'. Bohm suggests that this wave/particle complementarity can be explained by the implicate-explicate order duality. The implicate order consists of waves; the explicate order is rendered particulate.

Ultimately, underlying the implicate order is the "holomovement", an eternal multidimensional Ground resembling the Absolute Consciousness, or "One", of Neoplatonism. Thus, not only was the emergence of time and space, matter and energy given a causal base, so was the subjective consciousness of man. This view, while it replicates the knowledge of the mystic, and has the advantage of being a consistent and plausible model, also has the disadvantage, from the standpoint of science, of being wholly undemonstrable. But Bohm was more interested in a correspondence with truth than with a correspondence with scientific criteria.

We may readily recognize that the "implicate order" refers to what the mystic describes as the creative Energy of God out of which all phenomena arise, and in which all are implicit. At the root of this creative Energy is the all-blissful Consciousness that is God. While remaining ever-free and clear, He extends Himself by way of this Energy to the entire universe. His wholly independent and blissful Self is inherent and implicit in His Energy, and so He fills all animate and inanimate beings, to varying degrees according to their evolution, with His own Consciousness and Joy. Thus, the manifested beings, who are the evolutes of His Energy, are able to know within themselves His being, His freedom, His Consciousness, His Joy. They are able to transcend in mind the limitations of the egocentricity imposed on them in the process of manifestation, and ascend in consciousness to the very being of God, knowing Him as their original and authentic Self.

In that ascension, they perceive the perfection of His universal manifestation in which all created things are linked in a wonderful unity of being and becoming. Like the atoms in a cresting wave, or in the flowering of a rose, they are welded together in a synchronous dance of movement toward their intended evolutionary culmination. How vast and perfect in every way is their dance! It is indescribably wonderful! In the mystic's vision the unfolding of the universe and all that that entails is seen to be a coordinated and integrated presentation wherein "all things move together of one accord;" and "assent is given throughout the universe to every falling grain." This vision is to be found also in David Bohm's expression of the implicate-explicate order of the universe. He sees the "holomovement" as the ultimate conscious Source of the implicate order, and the implicate order as the causal framework of the explicate order—the explicate order being merely a "reflection" of the implicate order. In the mystic's vision, as in Bohm's theoretical postulations, the question of causality, brought up by the 'Copenhagen Interpretation' of quantum physics, is laid to rest.

Ordinarily, when we seek for causes of isolated events or things, we settle arbitrarily on a preceding event or state which we designate as the cause of the present event or state. But, as scientific investigations tend to show, the internal web of relationships between events and between things is endless. From the point of view expressed by the mystics, and by David Bohm, isolated things and events are not caused by other things and events, but are rather linked in a complex web of relationships within a larger common Whole whose nature, determined by the implicate order, in turn determines the nature of those constituent things and events. In other words, the material reality is no longer thought to be the independent bits of which the Whole is constituted, but rather the other way around: the material reality is the Whole, the condition of which governs the functions and interrelations of all constituent parts within the Whole. The logical conclusion is that all local and non-local causes must be referred to the condition of the Whole, which must in turn be regarded as the effective cause.

Here is how Bohm and his co-author, Basil Hiley, explain, in a 1975 article, this understanding:

The world which we perceive cannot properly be analyzed into independently existent parts with fixed and determinate dynamical relationships between each of the parts. Rather, the 'parts' are seen to be in immediate connection, in which their dynamical relationships depend, in an irreducible way, on the state of the whole system (and indeed on that of broader systems in which they are contained, extending ultimately and in principle to the entire universe). Thus, one is led to a new notion of unbroken wholeness which denies the classical idea of analyzability of the world into separately and independently existent parts. We have reversed the usual classical notion that the independent 'elementary parts' of the world are the fundamental reality, and that the various systems are merely particular contingent forms and arrangements of these parts. Rather, we say that inseparable quantum interconnectedness of the whole universe is the fundamental reality, and that relatively independently behaving parts are merely particular and contingent forms within this whole. [10]

In this broad suppositional proposition, causality is seen to rest in the implicate order (and ultimately in the "holomovement" itself), its effect being the explicate order in all its manifestory effusiveness. Small-scale causes are deemed irrelevant, as they are merely expressions of an implicit order. And, while this 'ontological interpretation' of David Bohm's is a marvelous restatement of and extrapolation on the expressed vision of the mystic, it remains, from the standpoint of science, merely another speculative philosophy, unprovable by science's criteria of proof. Nevertheless, Bohm's work is ground-breaking proof that gnosis is a fruitful source for scientific investigation and understanding. Perhaps other scientists will follow the path he has shown, expanding on his vision, and bringing us closer to a science that corresponds with the declarations of revelation proffered by the gnostics.

THE TWO IN ONE

Look, the Source is one and all that is;
But It has imaged forth a second, this cosmic array.
Eternally the one great Mind exists alone;
Its universal picture-show comes and goes,
An image on the screen of time.

Eternally, even as the stars play out their birth and death,
The One is undiminished, undivided, undismayed.
For, since the universal drama exists within the one great Mind,
There is no separation, no duality at all.

And yet, while we live and dance in time and space,

We inhabit an imaginary bubble of non-eternity,
Of transient bodies and volitional activities,
A secondary world, unreal.

For "real", by definition, refers only to the Permanent,
The Eternal, the Mind unmanifest and clear.
So what is this unseemly show, this conjured art,
This Mind-dreamt castle-in-the-air
In which we're sentenced to abide?

Alas, it's smoke and mirrors, a magic show,
Designed to reveal its Source to man.
For the fact is we've never left our eternal realm;
We delight there even now.

The timeless Self we know as "we" was never
Imprisoned in a bodily shell;
That's but an illusion, a paltry spell that binds us
To the dream of separate personality.
Once freed of duality's deception,
We realize we've never left eternity's bliss.
We're one eternal Self, unbound, unsnared forever,
Complete in the completion of the boundless One,
A "we", an "I" that stands triumphantly free,
beyond imagined time.

5

THE INTERCONNECTEDNESS OF ALL THINGS

There are two things I have come to believe implicitly about the world we live in. One is that nothing occurring in it is independent of any other thing; the other is that nothing that occurs is entirely random and prey to chance. These two beliefs are part of the same insight: if all occurrences are linked in some way with all others, everything acts in some way on everything else. Nothing happens in a purely random way. [11]

–Ervin Lazlo

Bohm's vision is, in its essence, compatible with, and partially identical to, the perennial vision of the mystics. It is flexible enough to encompass consciousness, creativity, and all the extrapolated phenomena experienced in the subjective and objective world of experience. It provides as well the answers to nearly all of the questions put forth by quantum physics in recent times; in fact, it was designed by Bohm to answer these questions. For example, the question regarding the phenomena of non-local effects: "non-locality" refers to the fact that particles from a larger particle that are split off from one another are able to affect one another immediately even at great distances—hence acausally as well as non-locally. Since there is no actual causal relationship between such distant particles, these non-local interactions are considered to be "synchronous", representing instantaneously connected ripples in a vast conscious ocean of energy.

Thus, all things, as projections of a higher dimensional reality, are immediately linked in a web of relationship which is not determined by proximity, or interacting forces, but simply by participation in that common conscious Whole. That distinct entities need not share the same local region of space to be immediately interconnected is therefore explained by Bohm's theory. As Bohm has stated:

> Ultimately, the entire universe (with all its particles, including those constituting human beings, their laboratories, observing instruments, etc.) has to be understood as a single undivided Whole, in which analysis into separately and independently existent parts has no fundamental status.[12]

This explanation of the acausal interconnectedness of particles that are constituents within a whole also suggests an explanation for clairvoyance, telepathy, and the oft-experienced phenomenon of synchronicity in human events, first given attention by Carl Jung. This refers to the occurrence of unexplainable and causally unconnected, yet meaningful, "coincidences" such as the type all of us have at times experienced. It may involve thinking of someone who then immediately calls on the phone. Or it may involve the uncanny repetition of a theme or motif in our daily life, such as an image, name or number repeatedly appearing in various circumstances. Or it might be evidenced in the actuality of some occurring event that you had dreamed of the night before. Such "coincidences" are explained similarly in terms of the quantum interconnectedness of all things in both the implicate and the explicate orders.

On the cosmic and the human scale, "synchronicity" refers to the universal propensity of matter and consciousness to follow a specific governing energy pattern: what Jung called an "archetype". *Archetype* is the name given to specifically defined "energies" which exist as invisible real-world "forces" that manifest in both the material and the mental realm. For example, the Sun, Moon, and the planets all have "archetypal" energies associated with them. These energies were described and elaborated into metaphorical personalities by earlier civilizations, namely the Babylonians and the Greeks, who regarded them as "gods", embodied as the planets. Thus, each of the bodies within the solar system, including the Sun and Moon, individually embody an archetypal energy which is said to define its particular "influence". These archetypal influences continue to exist today, even though we no longer think of them as "gods".

Many events which we would normally think of as synchronistic, or coincidental, occur in a common astronomical milieu; i.e., under common planetary conditions, as, for example, a retrograde station of Mercury, a Moon-Neptune square aspect, or any other similar configuration occurring in the heavens. A violent dream might occur at the exact time of a Mars transit to the position of a planet in our own personal natal planetary map. This would constitute a synchronistic relationship between the Mars' transit and our own psyche. However, most of us are unaware of the continuous angular interrelationships between planets or of their relationship to our own natal maps. And while many hold that such interplanetary relationships are not the *causes* of earth-events or psychological states, they are synchronous with them, and serve to signal the presence of archetypal energies operating in the external universe for those who are prepared to read these signs.

How, one wonders, do the planetary positions and angular relationships relate to human subjects? And most especially, how do the current positions of planets and their angular relationships relate to the positions of the planets at the time of the birth of the individual? Most scientists would answer, 'They don't. Such a notion is simply a relic of ancient superstition!' But the reality of the synchronicity of planetary positions and their archetypal energies with actual events or states of consciousness is unquestionable to one who has made a long and careful study of the planetary motions and their synchronous correlations. And yet the question of *how* these distant planets can affect a significant change in one's world and in the subjective content of one's mind is still an open question, and a matter of yet unresolved controversy. Is the connection local or non-local? Is it causal or acausal?

The theory of a local connection, adhered to by some, derives from the classical mechanistic view of the universe, and suggests some kind of wave pattern interference or facilitation. If there is an electromagnetic-type of wave field that extends from all the planets to earth and also interacts with human brain waves, then the connection is local, and the phenomena of astrological correspondences is explained as a *causal* relationship. To date, however, no such field has been discovered. The alternative theory is that mind and planets are instantaneously interconnected *non-locally* and acausally as embodiments of one all-pervasive Intelligence. Such correlations exist not in any cause-effect manner, but rather in the same way as the other acausal connections we have discussed; they exist because of the interconnectedness of all things within the universe at the "implicate" level. If this is true, we would never be able to know or prove *how* such correlations work; we could only say, "Thy will be done." According to this theory, the universe is not a great clock; it is one conscious and coordinated Whole established in the one great Mind.

According to this theory, it is a consciously projected and integrated Thought-construct in which we live; a dream-world. The planets and their synchronicity with mental and physical actions are, like us, constituents in an integral Thought-drama. Who can measure the relationships between items in a dream? They are not separate; they are constituents of a Whole, in which there are no divisions. It's all God - His Thought-projection. He is both the Cause and the effect. Within this Thought-drama, planets move, people evolve; it's all organically coordinated, but there are no independent causal relationships going on within it. It is the way it is because that is just the way He thought it, willed it. In other words, the planets are to be seen as signs, or markers, of particular archetypal energies contained within the whole, signifying elements of the cosmic design fashioned by a transcendent Intelligence. In such a universe, what clearer understanding could one gain by pursuing the matter further? Additional scientific enquiry would be irrelevant. Communing with the Author through love would be far more fruitful.

The dawning recognition by many scientists of the quantum interconnectedness of everything in the cosmos is one of the most significant recent developments within the scientific community. And one of the most potent sources of evidence for this view has recently been produced by Richard Tarnas, a cultural historian and professor of philosophy, whose book, *Cosmos And Psyche*, gives lucid and dramatic expression to one particular facet of this wholistic view. In his book, he relates the results of the thirty-years of research he accumulated on the relationships between the ordered movements of the planets and the historical events and psychological states observed in our Western culture over the last two millennia. From this study, he concludes:

> I have become convinced, after the most painstaking investigation and critical assessment of which I am capable, that there does in fact exist a highly significant—indeed a pervasive—correspondence between planetary movements and human affairs, and that the modern assumption to the contrary has been erroneous. The evidence suggests not that the planets themselves cause various events or character traits, but rather that a consistently meaningful empirical correspondence exists between the two sets of phenomena, astronomical and human, with the connecting principle most fruitfully approached as some form of archetypally informed synchronicity. [13]

Drawing upon an enormous amount of research, which is divulged in the course of his book, Tarnas builds an impressively unassailable case for the above conclusion. He has shown by scientific methods that there is, indeed, a proven correlation between the recognized archetypal energies associated with the various planets and the manifestation of those energies in the lives and activities of humans on earth. I had attempted to show, in my book, *The Supreme Self*, that even the mystical experience, the union of soul and God, is seen to be signaled by particular planetary patterns, especially as those transiting patterns relate to the positions of the planets at the time of the individual's birth; and Tarnas' work now confirms and corroborates those findings.

What an extraordinarily remarkable and amazing discovery this is: that our lives, our births, our very thoughts, are intertwined with the planetary energies and their angular relationships to one another! I too have watched and wondered at the amazing synchronicity evidenced between the planets and my own inner and outer world for over thirty years, and I doubted that I would ever see a comprehensive presentation of empirical evidence for these synchronicities in my lifetime. But Tarnas has accomplished the impossible. For that, he will take his place among the giants. In this recently published book, Tarnas, one of the finest, most well-informed, minds of our time or any other, has shown in an overwhelming fashion the synchronous correlations between various planetary patterns occurring throughout history and the events and cultural motifs that have surfaced historically in human affairs. It seems almost certain to me that this book will be regarded in the future as a significant watershed in the intellectual and spiritual development of our Western culture. Whether the minds of average citizens are capable of the mental subtlety required for grasping and utilizing this knowledge in their lives remains yet to be seen.

Tarnas' monumental study does not omit the recognition of a noumenal Cause behind the many interconnections in the universe; in fact he acknowledges the limitations of a purely "scientific" engagement with the cosmos, and advocates a larger engagement that integrates science with spiritual vision:

Yet this larger engagement with the cosmos will require of us a profound shift in what we regard as legitimate knowledge. It will demand an initial act of trust in the possible reality of an ensouled cosmos of transformative beauty and purposeful intelligence. [14]

... The cosmos as a living whole appears to be informed by some kind of pervasive creative intelligence—an intelligence, judging by the data, of scarcely conceivable power, complexity, and aesthetic subtlety, yet one with which human intelligence is intimately connected, and in which it can consciously participate. [15]

Though Tarnas is clearly an exception, there is a tendency among many of the purveyors of the newly formulated synchronistic world-view to omit or entirely dismiss the concept of an ultimate intelligent Cause, immanent within Its own creation. Acausal connections within the Whole do not eliminate the requirement of a Cause for the Whole itself. We must not simply take the 'implicate order' to be an independent *a priori* substratum. There is a supreme ruler from whom the implicate order derives, who generated the universe and set it in motion, who is its efficient and its material Cause as well as its underlying order, and who permeates every particle of the Whole. He has been called by many names; "holomovement" is simply the latest. He is not merely the implicate order; He is the Cause of all that exists, and is the center of our intelligence, our creativity, our soul; He is our true and lasting Self. He cannot be seen or measured in any way; and so He is beyond the methods of science. He can be known only through His gracious Self-revelation—in other words, through gnosis. He is the One to whom we must look, and the One to whom we offer reverence and gratitude for all that we are and all that we enjoy. Yes, Virginia, there is a God; He does exist. He really exists! And yes, He is loving; He is full of kindness and joy, and He knows everything. I know; I have seen Him.

THOU ART LOVE

Thou art Love, and I shall follow all Thy ways.

I shall have no care, for Love cares only to love.

I shall have no fear, for Love is fearless;

Nor shall I frighten any,

For Love comes sweetly and meek.

I shall keep no violence within me,

Neither in thought nor in deed,

For Love comes peacefully.

I shall bear no shield or sword,

For the defense of Love is love.

I shall seek Thee in the eyes of men,

For love seeks Thee always.

I shall keep silence before Thine enemies,

And lift to them Thy countenance,

For all are powerless before Thee.

I shall keep Thee in my heart with precious care,

Lest Thy light be extinguished by the winds;

For without Thy light, I am in darkness.

I shall go free in the world with Thee —

Free of all bondage to anything but Thee;

For Thou art my God, the sole Father of my being,

The sweet breath of Love that lives in my heart;

And I shall follow Thee, and live with Thee,

And lean on Thee till the end of my days.

6

THE CONSTANCY OF THE WHOLE

Which 'comes first', atoms or universe? The answer is 'neither'. The large and the small, the global and the local, the cosmic and the atomic, are mutually supportive and inseparable aspects of reality. You can't have one without the other. ...There is a unity to the universe ... It is a unity which says that without everything you can have nothing. [16]

—Paul Davies

David Bohm introduced us to the unbroken Whole, but this Whole cannot be known empirically. It is, however, experienced by the mystic, who tells us that the Whole is experienced in "the mystical vision" as a constant. From the perspective of the individual consciousness lifted to union with that creative Energy whose Source is the one pure Consciousness, and seeing with the eye of the Eternal, the totality emanating from the creative Energy of God is both in flux, and is constant: for one lifted to that vision, "all motion has ceased; everything continues." Though there is movement and change taking place within it, from the vantage point of the totality, the Whole, there is no movement, no duality of clashing worlds opposed; it is all one silence. From the perspective of Eternity, the Whole indeed remains one and constant. As the

Upanishadic seer said: "It moves. It moves not."

How can we understand this? Let us look to science for the answer in the First Law of Thermodynamics: as originally formulated, the First Law, also known as the Law of the Conservation of Energy, stated that, "the sum of the energy contained within a closed system remains constant." What, then, is a closed system? It is any operative energy system which neither depends upon energy from, nor transfers energy to, any system outside itself. A closed system, in other words, is a "perpetual motion machine" in which the energy produced is completely reutilized to power the system. Imagine, for example, a gasoline engine so enclosed that its energy-output was somehow transformed back into fuel to keep it running eternally without any loss of energy. That would be a closed system. Obviously, such a thing is not possible. There will always be some loss of energy, through friction, heat-loss, etc., to the surrounding environment. There is only one genuine closed system in existence – and that is the all-inclusive Whole. The Whole is the only closed system because it is everything; there is nothing outside it to which energy could be lost. If we consider the universe alone, it cannot be said to be a closed system, since it receives an influx of energy and consciousness from its Source and eventually returns to its Source. Only the entirety of existence, the Whole, may be considered a closed system.

A conservation Law identical with the one for energy was formulated to apply to mass, stating: "The sum of the mass within a closed system is constant." But not until Einstein made it clear that the two terms, *mass* and *energy*, were interchangeable, were the two Laws combined into one to state: "*The sum of the mass-energy within a closed system is constant.*" It is this Law which makes possible the rational demonstration of the constancy of the Whole. This Law, the Law of mass-energy conservation, asserts that, despite the incessant transformation of mass to energy, energy to mass, that occurs throughout the entire spectrum of existence, the sum, the totality, remains constant, unchanged – in essence, outside of time and space. In effect, this Law acknowledges an entity: *the sum*, the Whole, as a distinct entity over and above its constituent parts which possesses a quality that does not exist in its constituents: that quality is constancy. We see therefore that the Whole is something more than, and different from the aggregate of its parts.

We may at first find it difficult to conceive of the one Reality as an unchanging constant, since there is seen to be so much change taking place within it. But, if we consider the One, both in Its manifest and unmanifest states, as a Whole entity, then we must see that It does remain constant, since there is nothing in relation to which It can change. We may find it equally difficult at first to conceive of the Whole as unmoving, since it contains so much movement within it. Still, since there is nothing else in relation to which Reality as a Whole can move, it is unmoving. Only the One has this quality of 'all-ness' and therefore of constancy; and because there is nothing else like It to which It can be compared, we find it difficult to grasp with our minds just what It could be like. Nonetheless, the statement that "the Whole remains constant" expresses a very profound truth about the nature of the One. Remember, the universal Energy, which is manifest as the universe, is God's Energy; it is a projection of Himself, revealing Himself to Himself. And, though that Energy appears in the guise of myriad transformations and interactions within itself, it exists in its own constant and eternal mode, within God. That Energy is integral to the One Consciousness, and cannot be separated from It.

The constancy of God and His Energy is a truth that is corroborated by the mystics who have seen it. Jnaneshvar, the celebrated 13th century Indian mystic, speaks of it in the personal form, as "He":

> Though gold may be wrought into many ornaments, its 'gold-ness' never changes. In the same way, He never changes, though the universe contains so many forms. [17]

In fact, He remains constant whether there is a universe or not. He remains constant when the universe is expanding; He remains constant when it is contracting; He remains constant when there is no universe at all. He is the same constant Self even when the universal manifestation is only latent potentiality.

Let us make an analogy of the ocean: imagine that the ocean is infinite; if we regard its 'water-ness', the ocean is one whole, and is constant. But if we regard its 'wave-ness', the ocean is multiformed and incessantly changing. Now, one may say that only the water is real because it is the constant substratum, and the waves are unreal because they are merely ephemeral forms. But another, who fails to recognize the ground state, 'water', and sees only the waves, may say that only the incessant motion of the waves is the reality, and the idea of a permanent underlying reality is only conjecture. A wise person, intervening, might point out to both parties that the ocean has a dual-sided nature. It is always the whole body of water, and is therefore a constant; and it is also the moving forms of the water known as 'waves', and is from that viewpoint changing and inconstant.

Similarly, though a vast array of activity is occurring within the manifested universe, and there is a continual influx and replenishment of conscious Energy from the creative Power of the One, from the standpoint of the One, who inexhaustibly contains everything, nothing is happening; all motion has ceased, though all is still in motion as before. The One is eternally constant. A simple experiment will illustrate how this is possible: Shut your eyes; become aware of yourself as a single conscious entity. You will experience 'you' as a complete and undivided being. Now, shift your awareness to your body, becoming aware of the billions of cells being born, living and dying within you in every fraction of a moment. From this viewpoint, 'you' do not now seem so single, so indivisible. Yet, there are not two of 'you', but only one. It is similar to the mystic's experience of the constancy of the Whole, while simultaneously experiencing the continuance of the motion and activity taking place within the Whole.

"All things move together of one accord; assent is given throughout the universe to every falling grain." This is the vision of the mystic from a vantage point beyond time. But all things are moving together, not in a deterministic sense, but in an organic sense — as an Intelligence-guided, creative evolutionary unfoldment; much the way a flower's blossom unfolds or the way a drop of water in a cresting wave interacts with all the other drops to form the entire wave. We too are parts of the Whole, and creatively evolve both physically and consciously. Ultimately, we will become aware of our identity with the Source, and know our true freedom and Joy as the one Self of all, even while manifesting as individuals within this phenomenal manifestation that is the universe.

SONG OF PRAISE

O God, let me sing a song to Thee. I am just
Thy foolish unworthy child, as Thou dost know; but I beg Thee, let
me honor Thee with my song of praise. After all, I have no other
reason for existing but to sing Thy praise.

O God, Thou art so far beyond my vision that I do not know how
to begin to praise Thee. Thou art hidden beyond this world of my
daily experience, invisible to my eye. But Thou hast shown Thyself
to me when I was young. I know Thy perfect aloneness, untouched
by all that transpires here below; I know Thy timeless face, Thy
incomparable peace. Dear Lord, I can only stammer and write
these miserably inadequate words; for no words are there to speak
of Thee.

All that flows from Thee bespeaks Thy bounty; but Thou art far
greater than the sparkling sky, the star-filled cosmos. Thou art the
emptiness from which all bounty flows; an emptiness that contains
nothing, yet gives being to everything.

As winds arise from air, as waves arise from the sea, as dreams
arise from the quieted mind, so does the universe arise from Thee.
Thou art the bearer of happiness, the stirrer of devotion, the inven-
tor of thought, surprise, and awe. Thou art the redeemer of error,
the mother of love; Thou art the beauty of a summer's day. O God,
whatever is is done by Thee.

But why should I remind Thee of Thy works?
It is Thee, above all works, whom I adore.

I, who am Thy errant child, whose soul is birthed by Thee, and who longs to return to Thy womb, am nothing else but Thine own. Displayed into this world, I am Thy own substance, Thy own imagined form. And as I'm from Thee, so to Thee shall I return.

No longer image shall I be, but transformed into Thee, not something other, but Thee entire, one glowing I, unending, perfect beauty, perfect bliss, and consciousness absolute. None of these words, of course, come close to saying what Thou art; though I searched, I could not find words that tell Thee truly.

Down here, we have no words to describe what Thou art; and so, once more, my praise falls short. But we both know Thy true condition; we both know Thy unspeakable place of being; and we both know it is of that I speak. Dear Father of my life, my thought, my love, please accept my pitiful attempt to praise Thee. Fault me not for my lack of words that tell Thee. Only grant that I may always love Thee, till I'm once again at home with Thee.

O dear God of Gods, hear my prayer! You know my heart, my heart's desire: I long to rise above this worldly self to bathe in Thy untroubled Life. I cannot do it, but only Thou canst bring me there to live in Thee. O Lord, who art alone, sole Source and Master of the world, I beg Thee draw my mind and heart to Thee; let no other love distract me. Let no dreams or other goals detain me from my journey home to Thee.

7

THE UNITY OF GOD

Surely someday, we can believe, we will grasp the central idea of it all as so simple, so beautiful, so compelling that we will all say to each other, 'Oh, how could it have been otherwise! How could we all have been so blind for so long!' [18]

—John Wheeler

The mystic perceives in his transcendent vision a unitary Reality that is wholly constant and undivided. It may be referred to as monistic or non-dualistic. And yet, It has the appearance of duality since, in that unchanging Consciousness, that undivided One, there is a creative Power, a Thought-energy that projects upon itself this dynamic universe. Here, in the following "Great Exposition" attributed to the gnostic, Simon Magus of Samaria, who was a contemporary of the Christian apostle, Peter, this mystically perceived duality-in-Unity is magnificently explained:

There are two aspect of the One. The first of these is the Higher, the Divine Mind of the universe, which governs all things, and is masculine. The other is the lower, the Thought (*epinoia*) which produces all things, and is feminine. As a pair united, they comprise all that exists.

The Divine Mind is the Father who sustains all things, and nourishes all that begins and ends. He is the One who eternally stands, without beginning or end. He exists entirely alone; for, while the Thought arising from Unity, and coming forth from the Divine Mind, creates [the appearance of] duality, the Father remains a Unity. The Thought is in Himself, and so He is alone. Made manifest to Himself from Himself, He appears to be two. He becomes "Father" by virtue of being called so by His own Thought.

Since He, Himself, brought forward Himself, by means of Himself, manifesting to Himself His own Thought, it is not correct to attribute creation to the Thought alone. For She (the Thought) conceals the Father within Herself; the Divine Mind and the Thought are intertwined. Thus, though [they appear] to be a pair, one opposite the other, the Divine Mind is in no way different from the Thought, inasmuch as they are one.

Though there appears to be a Higher, the Mind, and a lower, the Thought, truly, It is a Unity, just as what is manifested from these two [i.e., the universe] is a unity, while appearing to be a duality. The Divine Mind and the Thought are discernible, one from the other, but they are one, though they appear to be two.

[Thus,] ... there is one Divine Reality, [apparently] divided as Higher and lower; generating Itself, nourishing Itself, seeking Itself, finding Itself, being mother of Itself, father of Itself, sister of Itself, spouse of itself, daughter of Itself, son of Itself. It is both Mother and Father, a Unity, being the Root of the entire circle of existence. [19]

This marvelous exposition preserved by Hippolytus (d. ca. 235) in his *Refutation of Heresies* as a laughable example of Gnostic cosmology, is in fact one of the most perfect examples of the non-dualistic view of reality expressed by mystics of any persuasion. Allow me to comment on it paragraph by paragraph:

> There are two aspects of the One. The first of these is the Higher, the Divine Mind of the universe, which governs all things, and is masculine. The other is the lower, the Thought (epinoia) which produces all things, and is feminine. As a pair united, they comprise all that exists.

In the mystical union with God, the mystic experiences the Eternal. He knows It as the One, without a second. He is one with It, and knows It as his own greater identity. There is no separation between the knower and the known. It is pure Consciousness, the "Divine Mind", aware of Its solitary existence. It is beyond time and space, beyond all movement or activity, and beyond every pair of opposites. It has been symbolized in the most ancient of religious literatures as "masculine", as "He", even though there is, of course, no gender inherent in It. This is to differentiate It from Its creative Power, Its power of "Thought", which is symbolized as female. Together, they constitute the "Father" and "Mother" of all things.

The creative Power of God is inherent in Him – as the power of thought is inherent in the mind of man. The Divine Mind, Itself, is the Ground; like the mind of man, It is consciousness, latent with thought, but other than the thoughts It produces. The creative Power is said to be the "lower" of the two aspects because it is produced from the Divine Mind. The Divine Mind is the independent Reality; the Thought is not independent, but has its source in the Divine Mind. It is the creative Power, the "Thought", that produces all that is in the universe, but it is *His* creative Power, and is not an independent entity. The two (who are really one) are therefore said to be the sum of reality, comprising all that exists.

This symbology, of male and female, is a mystical convention that dates from the earliest times, and may be found in almost every religious tradition. We see it today most especially in the "Hindu" religious tradition, where for several millennia representations of these two "aspects" of Divinity have been produced in the form of statues, paintings, and carvings, as well as in the vast religious literature of India. This figurative representation has often been taken to be a literal one, especially by the uneducated majority; but masculine and feminine in relation to God are conceptual symbols only, intended to differentiate the two aspects of the One. The various figurative representations of God as masculine and feminine, whether as *Shiva* and *Shakti, Vishnu* and *Lakshmi, Purusha* and *Prakriti*, and so on, bear no literal correspondence whatever to God, as He is formless and therefore infigurable. Nonetheless, the designation of the two aspects of God as masculine and feminine is an ancient and useful shorthand metaphor which serves as a means of distinguishing the absolute from the relative aspect of God, and which Simon Magus here utilizes.

The Divine Mind is the Father who sustains all things, and nourishes all that begins and ends. He is the One who eternally stands, without beginning or end. He exists entirely alone; for, while the Thought arising from Unity, and coming forth from the divine Mind, creates [the appearance of] duality, the Father remains a Unity. The Thought is in Himself, and so He is alone. Made manifest to Himself from Himself, He appears to be two. He becomes "Father" by virtue of being called so by His own Thought.

"Father" has been a designation for God since the beginning of time, for, of course, he "fathers" all that exists on the phenomenal plane. Our lives are born in Him, nourished and sustained by Him. He is "Father" because He is called so by us, His children, the products of His own Thought. He is Eternity; time and space exist only in the product of His Thought, but not in Him. His existence is of a kind unimaginable by the human mind. And, even though He is thought of as having two aspects, the male and female; He is never truly divided. The universe, which is the product of His Thought, does not go out from Him, but is contained within Him, as our own thoughts are contained within ourselves. Therefore, He is always One, and alone.

Since He, Himself, brought forward Himself, by means of Himself, manifesting to Himself His own Thought, it is not correct to attribute creation to the Thought alone. For She (the Thought) conceals the Father within Herself; the Divine Mind and the Thought are intertwined. Thus, though [they appear] to be a pair, one opposite the other, the Divine Mind is in no way different from the Thought, inasmuch as they are one.

To state, as some have done, that it is She, the Thought, which has produced the universe, and that He, the Divine Mind, is exonerated from all responsibility for this act, is to ignore the fact that it is *His* Thought, that it is *His* power which has produced the universe and all that is in it. She is inseparable from the Divine Mind, being His instrument. We, therefore, are constituted of His Thought; the Divine Mind and His Thought may not be considered to be separate in any way. It was in the interest of stemming this kind of dualistic thinking that the Hebrew scriptures (*Second Isaiah*: 45:4-7) put these words in the mouth of God: "I am the one Lord; there is no other beside Me. I form the light and create the darkness; I make peace and create evil. I, the one Lord, do all these things."

Though there appears to be a Higher, the Mind, and a lower, the Thought, truly, It is a Unity, just as what is manifested from these two [the world] is a unity, while appearing to be a duality. The Divine Mind and the Thought are discernible, one from the other, but they are one, though they appear to be two.

In the mystical experience, one experiences his identity with the Divine Mind, which is unmoving and unchanging; but he also experiences the "outflow" of the creative Power manifesting as the initiation of the universal appearance, its sustained appearance, and its subsequent withdrawal. This "projection" of the universe does nothing to diminish or in any way affect the Unity of God; but, for us mortals, clothed in body and spirit, it provides some difficulty in our speaking of it. The Divine Mind (God) contains no activity or change; all activity and change exist in the manifestation of the Thought; therefore, in order to speak of the constant activity and change in the phenomenal world of time and space, we must differentiate between the two aspects of God, and attribute activity and change to the Thought alone, and not to the Divine Mind. But they are a Unity still. Our own thoughts are produced from our consciousness, and have a life of their own, quite different from the consciousness which produced them. Still, they must be linked back to the consciousness from which they arose, having consciousness as both their efficient and their material cause. They are one, but they appear to be two.

> [Thus,] … there is one Divine Reality, [conceptually] divided as Higher and lower; generating Itself, nourishing Itself, seeking Itself, finding Itself, being mother of Itself, father of Itself, sister of Itself, spouse of Itself, daughter of Itself, son of Itself. It is both Mother and Father, a Unity, being the Root of the entire circle of existence.

There is one Divine Reality, which includes Its Thought, this universe and the many lives which exist within it; and though we divide it up with our language, conceptually separating thing from thing, person from person, It is a unity still. The Divine Mind, having spread Himself out into the world and all beings and nourishing them all with His life breath, is therefore nourishing Himself. As each being seeks Him, it is really God manifest as man who is seeking Himself, and finding Himself. As a mother, He gives birth to Himself; as a father, He spawns Himself. He is His own sister, wife, daughter, and son. As the Divine Mind, He is the Father; as the creative power – the Thought –, He is the Mother. He is ever One, being both the Root and all the branches of existence.

NONE ELSE

When you're drawn up to the One,

You'll find yourself alone.

There's no female at His side;

No attending angels round about.

There's no Son sitting nearby;

And no congregation of saints standing there.

Even "He" is not there.

Only You are there.

Not this little form of you;

But You as you never knew you were,

A nothing Mind, containing all.

Nothing else is there but You.

There is no Shakti there but You;

There is no Shiva there but You.

Purusha as well as Prakriti are You.

The throngs of souls are You;

The powers that be are You.

Wherever You look,

You see none else but You.

"Alone at last!" You sigh.

If there is to be an other,

You must imagine him or her.

The universe you project is You;

And all the people in it are You.

There's only ONE, and You are it.

The devotees who chant the name are You;

The universal choir of angels, You.

Whatever is is You, conjured by You.
There's none else but You anywhere.
In such a lonely timeless life,
What else is there to do but dream
Up worlds and populate them
With imaginative forms caught up
In crazy, impossible plots and toils?
What else would You do
When there's none else but You?

8

THE ETERNAL RETURN

If the universe is closed, the future is spectacular. In another 40 to 50 billion years, expansion will come to a halt and the universe will fall in on itself. ...Galaxies will rush toward each other, the cosmic background microwave radiation will be compressed, and the light will be shifted toward the visible. In time, the sky will blaze with light. Then stars and planets will melt into a universal soup of hot particles. The "Big Crunch" will continue until there is nothing but an empty universe: a space-time singularity at infinite temperature. [20]

—Herbert Friedman

From the beginning of time, men have speculated on the beginning and possible end of the universe. Scientists today acknowledge the expansion of the universe, shown by the red shift of the Doppler spectrum evident in the light of faraway stars, which indicates their increasing advance from us. These scientists are not yet certain, however, whether or not the universe is open or closed; that is, whether there is enough mass in the universe to ensure a reverse of its present expansion or not. So far, scientists have suggested that, from all observations, it seems there is not enough mass to make it a closed universe; but some believe that the missing mass may yet be discovered to lie in the dark matter which pervades the universe. At present, for scientists, the matter is an open question. For mystics, however, the question has been answered. They have seen in their union with God that the universe expands from its initial impetus in the creative Energy to a culmination of outward movement; and then it reverses its motion, returning to its initial state of rest as latent potentiality in the creative Energy. This cycle of expansion and contraction repeats itself over and over, without apparent end.

This expansion and contraction of the universe (sometimes referred to as "the eternal return") has been seen and reported by mystics for millennia. We find no mention of it in the Judaeo-Christian scriptures, but it is found in many of the Indian scriptural writings, as well as in the writings of many Western seers of antiquity. Here is how it is described in the *Svetasvatara Upanishad*:

He [the Lord] spreads his net [of appearance] and then withdraws it again into His *Prakriti* [His creative Power].[21]

And here, from the *Maitri Upanishad*:

The supreme Spirit is immeasurable, inapprehensible, beyond conception, never-born, beyond reasoning, beyond thought. He is vaster than the infinity of space.

At the end of the worlds, all things sleep: He alone is awake in eternity. Then from his infinite space new worlds arise and awake, a universe which is a vastness of thought. In the consciousness of Brahman the universe exists, and into Him it returns.[22]

In the 5th century B.C.E., the author of the *Bhagavad Gita* also discussed the process of manifestation-demanifestation in the following passages:

> They who know that the vast day of Brahma (the personified creative Power), ever lasts a thousand ages; and that his night lasts also a thousand ages—they know in truth day and night.
>
> When that day comes, all the visible creation arises from the Eternal; and all creation disappears into the Eternal when the night of darkness comes.
>
> Thus the infinity of beings which live again and again all powerlessly disappear when the night of darkness comes; and they all return again at the rising of the day.
>
> But beyond this creation, visible and invisible, there is a higher, Eternal; and when all things pass away, this remains for ever and ever. [23]
>
> Then Krishna, who is identified with the Eternal, says:
>
> At the end of the night of time all things return to my [creative Power, called] *Prakrti*; and when the new day of time begins, I bring them into light.
>
> Thus through my *Prakrti* I bring forth all creation, and these worlds revolve in the revolutions of time.
>
> But I am not bound by this vast work of creation. I exist alone, watching the drama of this play.
>
> I watch and in its work of creation *Prakrti* brings forth all that moves and moves not: and thus the worlds go on revolving. [24]

What do the mystics of other traditions have to say?

Lao Tze, of the Taoist tradition of China, who lived in the 6th century B.C.E., also spoke of the universal creation/dissolution cycle:

> The myriad objects of the world take form and rise to activity, but I have seen THAT to which they return, like the luxuriant growth of plants that return to the soil from which they spring. [25]

And Chuang Tze, who lived in the 3rd century B.C.E., wrote:

> The visible world is born of the Invisible; the world of forms is born of the Formless. The creative Energy [Teh] is born from the Eternal [Tao], and all life forms are born of this creative Energy; thus all creation evolves into various forms.
>
> ...Life springs into existence without a visible source and is reabsorbed into that Infinite. The world exists in and on the infinite Void; how it comes into being, is sustained and once again is dissolved, cannot be seen.
>
> It is fathomless, like the sea. Wondrously, the cycle of world-manifestation begins again after every completion. The Eternal [Tao] sustains all creation, but It is never exhausted.
>
> ... That which gives life to all creation, yet which is, Itself, never drawn upon – that is the Eternal [Tao]. [26]

And, in another passage, Chuang Tze similarly describes his mystically perceived knowledge of the Source of the universe:

> The Eternal [the Tao] is the source of the activity of universal

manifestation, but It is not this activity. It is the Author of causes and effect, but It is not the causes and effects. It is the Author of universal manifestation and dissolution, but It is not the manifestation or dissolution. Everything proceeds from It, and is governed by It; It is in all things, but is not identical with things, for It is neither divided or limited. [27]

Only he who can see the Formless in the formed arrives at the Truth. [28] He rejoices in THAT which can never be lost, but endures forever. [29]

Heraclitus (540-480 BCE) adds his voice to the consensus:

What is within us remains the same eternally; It is the same in life and death, waking and sleeping, youth and old age; for, It has become this world, and the world must return to It. [30]

This ordered universe...always was, is, and shall be, [like] an ever-living Flame that is first kindled and then quenched in turn. [31]

(This last, by the way, led unillumined commentators to say that Heraclitus believed the universe was made of fire.)

By all accounts, the creative expansion and "eternal return" of the universe to a state of potentiality in the Source was also recognized by Pythagoras (570-490 B.C.E.), Empedocles (495-435 B.C.E.), and the early Stoics, and was an established major tenet of Stoic meta-physics by the time of Plotinus, who said:

There is a raying out of all orders of existence, an external emanation from the ineffable One. There is again a returning impulse, drawing all upwards and inwards towards the center whence all came. [32]

Does anyone imagine that these mystics from diverse and widely separated cultures came upon this knowledge from a theoretical position? It was seen by each of them in union with the eternal Source. For the person who has "seen" this universal manifestation and demanifestation in its cyclic recurrence from the vantage point of Eternity, it is an unquestionable reality requiring no further affirmation; however, it will be gratifying when science, by its own methods, is able to confirm and support what the mystic already knows with certainty is true. He (the mystic) has seen its occurrence from the timeless state and observed its cyclic recurrence in the way one might watch his own breath being recurrently exhaled and inhaled.

It may be justifiably objected that this knowledge has little or no practical application to our spiritual understanding or practice. Since we live only a short while, and while living are concerned mainly for the felicity of our own existence during our brief tenure on earth, it seems of little use to know that, after billions of years, when humanity will have presumably reached its culmination (whatever that is), the universe will implode upon itself, and then eventually—after billions of more years—will begin the whole cycle of birth and death over again.

Indeed, it is a knowledge that serves little purpose in the abstract. But it is the truth; and its certainty in the mind of one who has "seen" it gives a timeless and dispassionate perspective to all that he witnesses on earth. For those reading about it, it is merely metaphysics, a conceptual framework. But to those who have reached those infinite shores, it is a certainty bearing reminiscence of the homecoming in which all soul-satisfaction resides. It is the happy return of man to God, of the soul to its ever-abiding Self, in the eternal awareness of the world as Its own divine, yet transient, radiance.

This knowledge is universal; it is not science, but it is confirmable by gnosis. Is it not possible, then, for men of science to adopt this universal knowledge as a foundation for their own enquiry? Must these two modes of knowledge continue on separate unrelated tracks? What wondrous results might develop in the future from a cooperative, non-contentious melding of gnosis and science, where each confirms the other, broadening the scope of knowledge and solidifying an unassailable worldview?

Many scientists have come to the conclusion that science alone can never solve the problem of reconciling material states with subjective ones. They can only describe the material states. What is required is another, non-scientific framework of knowledge. Science can benefit from the knowledge put forth by authentic representatives of gnosis to extrapolate from it principles that are in accord with both realms of knowledge.

One wonders what such a synthesis might look like if science incorporated into its assumptions the knowledge put forth by gnosis. Starting from the gnostic premise that the universe is a production of an absolute Consciousness, and that its appearance is produced by the manifestation of the conscious creative energy inherent in It, how would that serve to illuminate the path of the scientist? How would it affect the subsequent observations of all the branches of science from cosmology to physics to evolutionary biology and psychology? And how would it serve to unite both science and gnosis in a common framework? We know that such an accommodation is possible as there have been a number of great scientists who have incorporated both gnostic and scientific principles in their mindset: men such as Newton, Einstein, Schröedinger, etc. They seem to have nonetheless remained scientists – and brilliant ones at that.

I am certain that there are many people in the contemporary world like myself who are able to accommodate in their worldview both gnosis and science; they seem, in fact, to be in the majority. Why then, one wonders, are there so many scientists so vehemently opposed to validating gnosis, and to the acceptance of mystically perceived truths? Is it because they are convinced that science possesses the exclusive right to "knowledge"? Why is science so resistant to the adoption of that "consistent and relevant philosophical background" of which Fritjof Capra speaks? Are they simply too habitually and egotistically closed up in their own empirically limited perspective to allow for the possibility of a noumenal reality at the root of all existence? One can't help feeling that there is an element of hubris involved.

Science is limited to the phenomenal world of time and space; gnosis transcends that world and is capable of coming face to face with the eternal Source of that world. Doesn't it make sense to relegate each mode of knowledge to its respective realm and regard each as valid partners in the search for knowledge? Gnosis provides a foundational basis for science; science provides a means for the practical confirmation of gnosis. Only by taking both means into consideration is it possible to frame a true and complete view of the entire range of existence.

Remember Einstein's observation that "Science without religion (gnosis) is lame; religion without science is blind"? I would state it the other way around: 'Science without religion is blind; religion without science is lame.' With this metaphor, we may as wise men, hoist the lame gnosis onto the shoulders of the blind science, so that gnosis may point out the way for science to travel and science may provide the means of advancement, the means of progress on the journey toward a complete and all-comprehensive grasp of the reality in which we live.

NOW, WHILE THERE'S STILL TIME

Now, while there's still time, call on God with a yearning heart!

How swiftly passes this busy life of occupations and obligations.

Too soon, the day is lost to inconsequential chores;

Too soon the months, the years, are lost to scattered aims and fruitless schemes.

Suddenly we awake one morning, and we're old and feeble, unable to make any effort at all.

And who knows when the end will come?

You may be certain it will come one day — Perhaps without warning, unannounced;

Perhaps while you walk, or sleep, or play;

Or in between the syllables of a word you start to say.

And when it comes, will your heart leap up and cry, "O glorious day!"?

Or will you beg for just a little time to set things right—the way you'd always hoped they'd be?

O friend, make now your heart to be as you would have it then.

O now, my friend, while there's still time, call on God with a yearning heart!

Lead your soul to Him who is your true and everlasting home.

He is your joy unlimited, your boundless satisfaction;
Your Lord, your Goal, your Life, your Self.

9

CONSCIOUSNESS

The question that arises here is that of whether or not ...
consciousness can be understood in terms of the notion
that the implicate order is also its primary and immediate
actuality. If matter and consciousness could in this way be
understood together, in terms of the same general notion of
order, the way would be opened to comprehending their
relationship on the basis of some common ground. Thus
we could come to the germ of a new notion of unbroken
wholeness, in which consciousness is no longer to be fun-
damentally separated from matter. 33

–David Bohm

Many scientists are presently under the impression that
consciousness is a product of material processes, though
they are unable to understand just how consciousness
"emerged" from the matter of the brain, and by what process it did so.
No wonder! Consciousness did not evolve from brains.
Consciousness is primary to all manifestation and all processes; it is
the primary reality. For the mystic at one with the Source,
Consciousness is the immediately evident quality of that absolute
Self, and it is inherent in the creative unfolding of all manifestation.
When an individual consciousness is merged into the One, it does not
become unconscious; it is just that it no longer has a separable indi-
viduality. Consciousness is continuous, but it is in that union a con-

sciousness divested of its self individuation. Prior to the expansion into universal Consciousness, it regarded itself as an individual soul, begging for entrance into that larger realm. But when suddenly it awakes to the absolute Self, it is still the conscious 'I', only it is free of the limitation of its previous illusion of separateness.

It is still 'I', but it is not the little 'I' of the ego-identification; it is an unbounded 'I', with no limiting qualities; and it is realized to be the one and only 'I' that illumines and underlies all possible 'I's. It is one's own Self as it has always truly been, beyond the illusory limitations it had assumed as a separate individual self. To the consciousness lifted to that awareness, there is no question of who and what that unlimited Self is: It is the pure and absolute Consciousness that fills the universe with Its variegated effervescence, and lives within its own dramatic play of forms. "I am the pulse of the turtle; I am the clanging bells of joy!" that Consciousness exclaims; "I am in the clouds and in the gritty soil; in pools of clear water my image is found." Here all is one being; and I am that one being. No separation exists anywhere. The soul and the body, considered to be its temple, are no longer separate. "Where is the temple?" that consciousness asks himself; "Which the imperishable, which the abode?" All that exists, including ones own body, is seen to be, in essence, the projection of the one Self, identical with that eternal Self.

Following my own experience of the One, I went outside and scooped up a handful of gravel. "I am in this?" I questioned. Thrust from the unitive awareness back into the phenomenal world of separate individuality, it was incomprehensible to my bewildered mind that all consisted of the one Consciousness that I had so clearly experienced as 'I'. But that is the truth! All is Consciousness. All that appears—mass, energy—all is Consciousness; though naturally there are gradations of awareness in this all-inclusive Consciousness. Nonetheless, all is made of and imbued with that one pure Consciousness. It is the undeniable Self of all that exists.

This unitive experience has been described numerous times in the scriptures of all religious traditions. It was undoubtedly the experience of Jesus, as evidenced in his declaration, "I and the Father are one", and forms the basis for all his teachings. It has been known by mystics throughout history, and has been told in many ways. It is only today, in the midst of our Western materialistic society, that it appears as a startlingly new and extraordinary fact. To be sure, such an experience occurs but rarely, and is therefore little heard of by the uninitiated populace; but the experience of Unity, and the knowledge (gnosis) derived from this experience, has begun to influence the way people think about the reality in which they live today. Science has gone far afield of this transpersonally acquired knowledge, and must now come to terms with it and reconcile its own theories of reality with the realizations of the gnostics.

Up till recently, Western civilization in general has been accustomed to thinking of the Judaeo-Christian tradition as the benchmark of "religion", yet it found little there to satisfy its craving for understanding of the world. After all, its scriptures date back 3000 years or more, and represent the knowledge of simple tribesmen of an agrarian age in a small corner of the world. Jesus was a mystic, and was murdered for the expression of his vision, and the religious organization that built itself around him suffers the errors common to all such popular organizations, comprised as they are of unillumined persons. Science, therefore, which promised an uncompromising investigation of truth through the method of empirical experiment, became the religion of this society, and was looked to for answers to the questions of the nature of life and reality. And now, with the worldwide spread of learning, the writings of the mystics are reaching more and more; and science too is forced to take into account the vision of reality they expounded.

This mystical vision is found to be well represented in the scriptures of the Eastern religious traditions, such as Taoism, Sufism, and most particularly in the esoteric branch of Hinduism called Vedanta. Vedanta presents a non-dualistic philosophy derived from the mystical vision of the authors of the Upanishads and the long list of enlightened commentators who came thereafter. Vedanta recognizes the transcendent unqualified Consciousness (*Brahman*) as identical with the Self (*Atman*) of all intelligent beings, and recognizes as well the delusive effect on those beings of the creative Power (*Maya*) that emanates from that one Consciousness in the process of manifesting the universe. Here, from "The Crest-Jewel of Discrimination" (*Vivekachudamani*), the eighth century sage, Shankara, explains that vision:

There is a self-existent Reality, which is the basis of our consciousness of ego. That Reality is the witness of the three states of our consciousness (waking, dreaming, and dreamless sleep). That Reality sees everything by its own light. No one sees it. It gives intelligence to the mind and the intellect, but no one gives it light. That Reality pervades the universe, but no one penetrates it. It alone shines. The universe shines with its reflected light. Its nature is eternal consciousness. This is the Self (*atman*), the Supreme being, the ancient. It never ceases to experience infinite joy. It is always the same. It is consciousness itself.

It is the knower of the activities of the mind and of the individuality. It is the witness of all the actions of the body, the sense-organs and the vital energy. It seems to be identified with all these, but it neither acts nor is subject to the slightest change. The Self is birthless and deathless. It neither grows nor decays. It is unchangeable, eternal. The Self is distinct from its creative Energy (*Maya*) and from her effect, the universe. The nature of the Self is pure consciousness. In and through the various states of consciousness— the waking, the dreaming and the sleeping—it maintains our unbroken awareness of identity. It manifests as the witness of the intelligence. [34]

The Self is the witness—beyond all attributes, beyond action. It can be directly realized as pure consciousness and infinite bliss. Its appearance as an individual soul is caused by the delusion of our understanding, and has no reality. By its very nature, this appearance is unreal. When our delusion has been removed, it (the soul) ceases to exist. [35]

… The Self is one with Brahman (God): this is the highest truth. Brahman alone is real. There is none but He. When He is known as the supreme Reality, there is no other existence but Brahman. Because of the ignorance of our human minds, the universe seems to be composed of diverse forms. But it is Brahman alone. Apart from Brahman, it does not exist. Our perception of it as having an independent existence is false, like the perception of blueness in the sky. No matter what a deluded man may think he is perceiving, he is really seeing Brahman and nothing else but Brahman. He sees mother-ofpearl and imagines that it is silver. He sees Brahman and imagines that it is the universe. But this universe, which is superimposed upon Brahman, is nothing but a name. [36]

Vedanta acknowledges the creative Power (*Maya*) of the one Consciousness that manifests as the universe, and stresses that its product, the universe, is merely a thought-projection of the one Consciousness and not that absolute Consciousness itself. It projects an energy that coalesces to form an "illusory" reality of transient forms on the formless Reality, which become the objects of the out-going senses that distract man from awareness of his true Self. It also produces a delusory effect upon the consciousness of man, creating the sense of an independent selfhood (the ego) which is difficult to overcome.

One day people will marvel that, even in the 21st century, the leading intelligentsia and guardians of scientific knowledge on this planet believed that this universe appeared willy-nilly by chance, organized itself into a life-supporting environment, and gave birth to sentient creatures, all in an accidental, undesigned manner; and that consciousness "emerged" of itself from the complexity of that chance material organization. What a marvelous testament to the veiling power of Maya and the delusion of the human ego! This Maya is said to be inexplicable, and we in this present century also find this creative Power and its projected world of matter and energy to be inexplicable.

Maya, in her potential aspect, is the divine Power of the Lord. She has no beginning (as she is inherent in the eternal One). She is neither being nor non-being, nor a mixture of both. She is neither divided nor undivided, nor a mixture of both. She is neither an indivisible whole, nor composed of parts, nor a mixture of both. She is most strange. Her nature is inexplicable.

... You must know that Maya and all its effects—from the cosmic intellect down to the gross body—are other than the Self. All are unreal, like a mirage in the desert. [37]

Science in the last two centuries has certainly convinced us of the illusory nature of what we call "matter". When Shankara says that the effects of Maya are unreal, he is taking as "real" only that which is eternal and unchanging—the Self. This does not imply, of course, that we are "unreal"; we are identical with the eternal reality. It is only the appearances that we tend to identify with that are non-eternal, and therefore unreal. In fact, Shankara stated as a compressed synopsis of his teachings the brief formula: *brahma satyam jagat mithya jivo Brahmaiva naparah*; "Brahman is the reality. The world is an illusion. The Self of man is truly Brahman." Brahman is the ultimate reality. He is realized in the experience of union with Him to be one's eternal Self.

We may speak of the "free choices" of individual egos and even of every quanta in a multitude of multidimensional universes, but the integrative Whole, the underlying "Reality" is Consciousness—the one absolute Consciousness in which everything lives and moves and has its being. All individualized entities and the amazingly complex drama in which they exist, and which unfolds in time and space, consists of that one Consciousness; and That, and That alone, is the ultimate and primary Reality.

The universe, as well as all possible subtle or gross universes, is in many ways similar to a dream. All is played out of necessity no doubt, but all manifestations are resolvable in the One, as an infinite number of waves are always reducible to the ocean on which they arise. We do not "return" to the Absolute; we can never leave It. We are *in* It, identical with It—always have been, and always will be; for It is the only and entire Reality. This is the central truth which we must hold as paramount through all our permutations and mental wanderings.

Brahman is supreme. He is the reality—the one without a second. He is pure consciousness, free from any taint. He is tranquility itself. He has neither beginning nor end. He does not change. He is joy forever. He transcends the appearance of the manifold, created by Maya. He is eternal, forever beyond reach of pain, not to be divided, not to be measured, without form, without name, undifferentiated, immutable. He shines with His own light. He is everything that can be experienced in this universe.

The illumined seers know Him as the uttermost reality, infinite, absolute, without parts—the pure consciousness. In Him they find that knower, knowledge and known have become one. The know Him as the reality which can neither be evaded (since He is ever-present) nor grasped (since He is beyond the power of mind and speech). They know Him as immeasurable, beginningless, endless, supreme in glory. They realize the truth: *aham brahmasmi*, "I am Brahman". [38]

THEY ASK ME

They ask me, "How can man and God be one?
It makes no sense; it can't be understood."
I answer, "He is all, and all are He!
No other exists but Him; so who are you?"

Becoming one with God is just the realization
Of what is and has always been true.
The self you think you are is only a mirage;
The Self you've always been is that eternal One.

We go about in our illusory shells,
Identifying with the dance of atoms,
A mere framework of form and ideas.
But only when He opens wide our inner eye
Is it revealed that we are Him and He is us.

This truth is not so easily perceived;
It's hidden by the power He wields.
And even when it's once revealed,
It's hard to hold; it slips away.

We pray, we concentrate our minds on Him,
And search our inner sky for that all-revealing Sun.
We shut out all distracting thoughts,
And open up our souls to Him.
Yet rarely does the clear light dawn
 That shows our own eternal face.
More often we rely on thoughts inspired

That come to us as wisdom from on high.

Our prayers, our yearning hearts, uplift us

 To that place where thought runs pure and clear;

And in this way we come to know His presence deep within.

But those who've gained His favor know a higher vision still;

His Grace reveals the truth of truths:

The Self of all is I!

They ask me, "How can man and God be one?"

I ask them, "In the Unity that is His all-inclusive Self, How can you imagine there are two?

 If nothing else exists but God,

Then who, on earth, are you?

10

THE SOUL

What if souls ... didn't just emerge out of creation fully formed but were actually created through the process of evolution in the same way that brains were? That would mean that the soul is not a permanent, ever-existing entity any more than a cell is a permanent, ever-existing entity. It has, instead, evolved over time and will continue to evolve in the future. ...That would mean that it's all—physical and nonphysical, material and immaterial, gross and subtle—part of one evolutionary process. [39]

–Carter Phipps

In the above exposition of Brahman by Shankara, there is little mention of the "soul" of man. Indeed, he regards the soul as a false and illusory predication of identity upon the Self which vanishes when the truth is revealed. And this is a true representation of the soul from my own perspective. But wait; let us examine more closely the question of the existence of souls: It seems to me that, despite the insistence by Buddhist philosophers and certain Advaita Vedantins that there is no such entity as an individual 'soul', there are a number of reasons to accept the existence of individual souls in the phenomenal realm, produced in the raying out of God's Power. Here are some of those reasons:

1. The soul, or *jiva*, is treated of in every religious and philo-

sophical tradition throughout history, including Platonism, Neoplatonism (Plotinus), Hinduism, Judaism, and Christianity. Christianity, for example, is unexplainable without the notion of individual souls. In the Hindu tradition, one finds extensive treatments of the nature of the individual soul in various Upanishads, like the *Svetasvatara* and the *Maitri*, as well as in the *Bhagavad Gita* (Chapter XV).

2. Soul is a logical necessity in the causal progression from absolute Consciousness to the existence of individual human entities. In order to be productive, the Creative Power of the One radiates the phenomenal (intelligible) universe, to be sure; but how are human individuals linked to Divinity, if there is no extension such as Soul? Else how came we to be? The projection of the Creative Power as Soul, becoming the plenitude of individual subtle, "astral" bodies, or souls, is not an unthinkable notion. Physical bodies exist in the phenomenal world; why not subtle bodies that incarnate as physical bodies? The mind is a non-physical entity, as are its products, whose existence no one calls into question; why not souls?

The great 3rd century mystic and philosopher, Plotinus, whose divine knowledge is far deeper than my own, and whose vision I honor, explained Soul as an emanation, or radiation, of the Creative Power (*Nous*) of the Divine. In terms of the sequence of causality, the unqualified One is primary, the Creative Power (*Shakti, Logos, Prakriti, Nous*) is secondary, and Soul is its product, the third phase of Divine manifestation, flowing outward in a manner similar to the outward radiation of the Sun's rays. Soul, according to Plotinus, is undivided at its Source, but appears as divided, as it becomes individually associated with diverse bodies. As Plotinus puts it,

> There is one identical Soul, every separate manifestation being that Soul complete.[40] The differentiated souls ... issue from the unity while still constituting, within certain limits, an association. They are one Soul by the fact that they do not belong unreservedly to any particular being; ...They strike out here and there, but are held together at the source much as light is a divided thing upon earth, shining in this house and that, while yet remaining uninterruptedly one identical substance." [41]

In another telling passage, Plotinus asks:

> May we think that the mode of the soul's presence to body is that of the presence of light to the air? This certainly is presence with distinction: the light penetrates through and through, but nowhere coalesces; the light is the stable thing, the air flows in and out; when the air passes beyond the lit area it is dark; under the light it is lit: we have a true parallel to what we have been saying of body and soul, for the air is in the light quite as much as the light [is] in the air." [42]

3. Another objection is that if there is no soul as a recurring entity, how may there be any continuing progress from lifetime to lifetime toward Self-knowledge? This contradicts the idea of soul-evolution, without which life consists for the overwhelming masses of people as a life-journey curtly interrupted, with no hope of resuming that journey toward its cul-

mination. In order for there to be karmic transfer from life to life, there must be an entity which bears the karma. Some proponents of Advaita Vedanta contend that karmas are redistributed randomly after death to newly born humans, and are not permanently associated with one particular being; but that seems to make no sense at all.

The position of some neo-Vedantists is that there is no soul, and no individual karma, but rather the karmas alone persist and are distributed randomly to new body-mind complexes indiscriminately as they are born. However, this is not a theory I can accept; it is illogical, and begs many questions in the face of evidence to the contrary. Now, granted that I am only theorizing about souls, I feel that the theory of soul is based on the evidence of logic as well as of my own and millions of others experiences in the phenomenal world.

4. The most compelling argument for souls is the testimony of the many who have "seen" and conversed with the souls (or ghosts) of departed loved ones. If these subtle level beings are not souls, what are they? Also, some people have separated from the physical body in trance-like states or "near-death experiences", and have moved about in that subtle state, later describing their activities and observations. If this is not the 'soul', what is it?

Let me tell you a story of my own experience:

In 1979, while I was living in a New York apartment across from the ashram where I taught as a swami, I awoke in the night with the distinct sense that someone was in the bedroom with me; an invisible someone who was very angry and threatening. I sat up and ordered this presence to get out of my room. By the power of my own soul-force, I commanded it to go, and it left. Shortly thereafter, I was again awakened with a call from the ashram, telling me that there was a phone call for me over there. I went over, and spoke to my father on the phone, who informed me that my mother had just died. When I returned to my apartment, the thought came to me that it had been my mother who had come to me earlier, and her anger was because I had not come to be with her during her illness. Somehow, I was able to call her back to me, and there ensued a touching reconciliation between mother and son, whereby I was able to assure her of my love. An additional glowing presence, who I was sure was my guru, was also there, and I watched as he lifted her on high and guided her, now free, to her "heavenly" destination. There was a great sense of gratification that all resentment had been assuaged between us, and that she had been guided to a "higher" place.

I believe this is not an uncommon experience. Such experiences have been described over the centuries by thousands of psychics, as well as ordinary sensitives, which suggest that souls do indeed exist. Souls (consisting of causal and astral bodies) are ephemeral entities appearing in the phenomenal world at a subtler level than the physical level, and have been described as such by the authors of the Upanishads, by Plotinus, by great sages such as Paramahansa Yogananda, whose spiritual authority I regard as unassailable, and by Divines of every persuasion. I feel the evidence is overwhelming.

However, in my own experience of union with the eternal One, there was no soul or souls present. The objection to the existence of individual souls usually comes from one who, like myself, has had a "mystical" experience, and has experienced first-hand the one eternal Self of all. In that experience, there is seen no individual soul, but only the one undivided Self is realized to be the Identity at the root of one's own and all manifested selves. It may be argued, however, that since the "mystical experience" is a direct union with the transcendent and eternal Consciousness, souls, therefore, which exist only at the phenomenal level, simply are not perceived there. The point to be made is that, despite the absence of souls in the unitive mystical experience, it should be recognized that that visionary experience is of the timeless Origin, the unmanifest Consciousness, wherein souls could not possibly exist. If souls are to come into existence, it must be only subsequent to the activity of the Creative Power, the details of whose activity I was not privy to in that unitive mystical experience.

The person who perceives the one eternal Self in a "mystical experience" knows for certain that he is that Self and nothing else. There is no evidence at all in that direct gnosis of an individualized soul. Indeed, the soul, which is identical with the ego, is of necessity vanished, if the Self is to be realized. But it is granted, by all who have experienced the eternal Self, that, along with the world of time and space, the ego-self returns when the experience of the Self wanes. That ego-self, it seems to me, is synonymous with 'the soul'. Otherwise, what is it?

I have come to the conclusion that, in the end, so long as one recognizes that, in the beginning, in the middle, and in the end, there is only God, it doesn't really matter philosophically whether the existence of souls in the phenomenal realm is accepted or not. If there are souls, which evolve toward their mergence in the One, the ultimate Reality is still the One Consciousness, the One Existence;

and souls are merely a transitory phenomenon within that One, like all other transient phenomena. If there are no souls, then there is only the One, appearing as many. The One is the same even when there is a plenitude of physical bodies; It is the same whether or not there is a plenitude of subtle bodies (souls) which exist for a time, evolve, and then become merged and dissolved in the One. The multiplicity of forms, subtle or gross, does not, in the slightest, nullify or reduce the unity, all-pervasiveness, and sole reality of the one Self.

God shines out as the universe of form; it is God at the beginning, and God in the middle, and God as the human body and consciousness. There are different "stages" or "levels" of His emanation, and we apply different names to each stage, such as "creative Power", and "Soul." But, clearly, there is nothing but God, doing what He does. If He had remained unproductive, content to remain unmanifest, we would not be here. But we are here, the universe exists; and we and it are evidence of His "emanation" of Himself into the realm of phenomena. His existence as conscious human entities, we call "Soul" or "souls". But, by the fact that we humans are able to "see" into our true nature, into our original being, and know that we are God, it is evident that "Soul" is just another name for God – in His extension as projected individuations.

In my book, *The Supreme Self*, (to which this may be considered a companion volume) I described this experience of enlightenment, wherein the Self was experienced by the Self, no intervening soul being present. Yet I felt it necessary to posit the existence of souls, at least as temporary superimposed phenomena prior to final mergence in the One; and I stick by this judgment. Here is an excerpt from that account:

To the philosophers and theologians of the West, the soul was conceived of as a concrete individual entity, which retained its individualized existence for all eternity. But in the East, the soul (or *jiva*) is regarded as identical with the universal Self—limited only by a false sense of individuality, or ego. This sense of individuality is regarded by Indian philosophers as a mere ignorance (*avidya*) of one's greater, universal Self. But this ignorance is not the ordinary kind of ignorance that can be easily remedied by the learning of facts; it is an ignorance that is "built-into" our human existence; in other words, it is an ignorance that is "God-given," and which can only be dispelled by His Grace, His Self-revelation. From this point of view, so long as the illusion of individuality exists, the soul exists; and only when this illusion is dispelled by the inner revelation of the universal Self, does the illusion of a separate soul cease to exist.

During the mystical experience of Unity, there is neither soul nor God, for that which imagines itself to be an individual soul becomes suddenly aware that it is the one and only Consciousness of the universe. In that pure Consciousness, there is no soul, no God; the polarization of subject-object exists only while the veil of ego-identification remains. This is not to say that the soul is unreal, a mere personal illusion, like a mirage; the soul is a manifestation of Divine Energy. If it is an illusion, it is an illusion produced by the supreme Consciousness; it is a product of His Divine Power of Illusion (Maya), and therefore is as real as any other of His manifestations. It continues its "illusory" existence for lifetime after lifetime, and ceases to exist only when He chooses to reveal

Himself." [43]

"We can only surmise that the process of individuation is the sport, or play, of the one Consciousness. But I do know one thing for sure: that the dawning of enlightenment, the vision of ultimate Unity, puts an end to the conceit of individuation, and what we call the soul; for the final truth is that there is only one I who is playing all the parts of all the souls. [44]

So, while we may find it fascinating to examine the many facets of our own unique soul, the truth is that all these characteristics are only temporary superimpositions on our one true and eternal Identity. The truth is 'I am the Self. I am Brahman'. Hear what Shankara says:

The fool thinks, 'I am the body'. The intelligent man thinks, 'I am an individual soul united with the body'. But the wise man, in the greatness of his knowledge and spiritual discrimination, sees the Self as [the only] reality, and thinks, 'I am Brahman'. [45]

I am that Brahman, one without a second, the ground of all existences. I make all things manifest. I give form to all things. I am within all things, yet nothing can taint me. I am eternal, pure, unchangeable, absolute.

I am that Brahman, one without a second. Maya, the many-seeming, is merged in me. I am beyond the grasp of thought, the essence of all things. I am the truth. I am knowledge. I am infinite. I am absolute bliss.

I am beyond action, the reality which cannot change. I have neither part nor form. I am absolute. I am eternal.

Nothing sustains me, I stand alone. I am one without a second.

I am the soul of the universe. I am all things, and above all things. I am one without a second. I am pure consciousness, single and universal. I am joy. I am life everlasting. [46]

DO YOU WISH TO KNOW GOD?

Do you wish to know God?

Then pray for His grace. But even that you cannot do

Until the magnet of His Love draws forth your heart's desire.

Do you wish to know God?

That wish is God's own power alive within you drawing you home.

But you must set your wings for flight and soar to heights

unknown before,

Releasing all below.

A strong and focused mind will be the wings on which you'll climb

to His domain

Where you may offer up your soul to Him and beg for entrance to

His heart.

If you are steady in your goal, His heart will open wide

and draw you in to reveal that you are one with Him.

And then you'll know that you and He were never set apart.

You'll see the universe in you; in you, the universal Self.

Your calling lifts you toward Him, but He responds only in His

time.

He will leave you yearning for His love, your heart an abject song;

For He tortures those who love Him with a longing unfulfilled,
And lures us on with sweetness, withholding His embrace.

What pathetic fools He makes of us who bargain all for Him,
Who fill our nights with lonely pleas that He might hear our song!
Addicts of His mercy, we pray He'll bring us home,
And fold us in His sweet embrace as a father does a son.

No doubt, His mercy keeps us there in longing for His touch;
Our hearts grow sweet, our love expands, as we call aloud His name;
And lift our minds and hearts to Him, desiring only Him.
This barb of sorrow, this aching love, upholds us in His grace,
And leads us upward, onward, till one day we shall see His face.

O, who will take me to my Lord? Who will give me wings?
I grow older, Father, every day, and my mind is growing dim.
My eyes are weak, my vision strains to penetrate the dark.
My Lord, I have no other goal but Thee; have mercy on this soul!

11

THE LOGOS

(The evidence) makes it seem more and more likely that reality is better described as mental than material... The universe seems to be nearer to a great thought than a great machine. [47]

—James Jeans

In ancient Greece, the word *Logos* was a common word for "thought" or "idea". Heraclitus (540-480) was one of the first to use the word to represent the Thought of God as it manifests in and as the phenomenal universe in which we live, constituting as well its ideational order. Heraclitus was a mystic who had "seen" God and who had "seen" into the nature of the universal manifestation; and he wrote a book called *On Nature*, in which he set down his knowledge of the Eternal and of Its manifested Thought. Today, we possess only fragments of his original book. Here is a reconstruction of some of those fragments:

I have explained the Logos, but men are always incapable of understanding it, both before they have heard it, and after. For, though all things come into being in accordance with the Logos, when men hear it explained—how all things are made of it, and how each thing is separated from another according to its nature—they seem unable to comprehend it.

The majority of men are as unaware of what they are doing

after they wake from sleep as they are when asleep. ...
Everyone is ruled by the Logos, which is common to all; yet,
though the Logos is universal, the majority of men live as if
they had an identity peculiar to themselves. ...Even when
they hear of the Logos, they do not understand it, and even
after they have learnt something of it, they cannot comprehend; yet they regard themselves as wise.

Those who believe themselves wise regard as real only the
appearance of things, but these fashioners of falsehood will
have their reward. Though men are inseparable from the
Logos, yet they are separated in it; and though they encounter
it daily, they are alienated from it. What intelligence or understanding do they have? They believe the popular orators, and
are guided by the opinions of the populace; they do not understand that the majority of men are fools, and the wise few.

Of all the wise philosophers whose discourses I have
heard, I have not found any who have realized the one
Intelligence which is distinct from all things, and yet pervades
all things. That Intelligence is One; to know It is to know the
Purpose which guides all things and is in all things. Nature
has no inherent power of intelligence; Intelligence is the
Divine. Without It, the fairest universe is but a randomly scattered dust-heap. If we are to speak with intelligence, we must
found our being on That which is common to all. ...For that
Logos which governs man is born of the One, which is
Divine. It [the Divine] governs the universe by Its will, and is
more than sufficient to everyone.

One should not conjecture at random about the Supreme.
The eyes are better witnesses to the truth than the ears; but the

eyes and ears are bad witnesses for men if their souls cannot understand. You could not in your travels find the source or destination of the soul, so deeply hidden is the Logos. [But] I searched for It [and found It] within myself. That hidden Unity is beyond what is visible. All men have this capacity of knowing themselves, [for] the soul has the Logos within it, which can be known when the soul is evolved. What is within us remains the same eternally; It is the same in life and death, waking and sleeping, youth and old age; for, It has become this world, and the world must return to It.

I'm going to stop for a moment here in order to explain to you what Heraclitus is telling us, in case it is unclear to you. He has clearly "seen" the Eternal and the projection of Its Thought as the universe. He's saying that this entire variegated world that we see is of the nature of Thought, that the world we walk and talk in is a Thought-construct in the Mind of God; and that, because of our blindness; we are unable to see it, to register this knowledge in our minds. Let us continue to hear what Heraclitus has to say:

The best of men choose to know the One above all else; It is the famous "Eternal" within mortal men. But the majority of men are complacent, like well-fed cattle. They revel in mud; like donkeys, they prefer chaff to gold. [The Eternal is attained only by those who seek It with all their desire;] for, if one does not desire It, one will not find the Desireless, since there is no trail leading to It and no path. Such a man is satiated with things seen, and kindles his inner light during the night. While living, he is like a dead man; while awake, he is like a man asleep. But such men, the best of men, are one in ten thousand.

You needn't listen to me; listen to the Logos [within]. When you do, you will agree that all things are One. This ordered universe, which is the same for all, was not created by any one of the gods or by man, but always was, is, and shall be, an ever-living Flame that is first kindled and then quenched in turn. [The universe bursts forth and then is reabsorbed, yet its Source is ever-living, like a Sun that never sets;] and who can hide from that which never sets? [That eternal Intelligence in man] is forever beyond change; [It is God.] To God, all things are beautiful, good and just, but men see some things to be just, and others unjust.

One should understand that the world appears by the opposition of forces; order exists in the world by this play of contraries. We would never have heard of "right" if we did not know of "wrong"; whole and not-whole, united-separate, consonant-dissonant—all these are interdependent. [But] in the One, above and below are the same, [just as] beginning and end are one in the circumference of a circle. That which is in conflict is also in concert; while things differ from one another, they are all contained in the most beautiful Unity.

This too is the universal experience of the mystic: he sees that his very ego-self, now vanished, was made up of duality; i.e., the pairs of opposites which manifest as the awareness of I-Thou, now-then, life-death, good-evil, and so on. But in the mystical experience of Unity, all these opposites are seen to be reconciled and accommodated, co-existing in the One. Here is the extant conclusion of

Heraclitus' revelation:

[Yet the philosophers cannot understand this;] they do not understand how that which contains differences within It is also in harmony, how Unity consists of opposing forces within Itself, just as the strings of a bow or a lyre [produce harmony by being pulled by opposing forces].

[When one's mind becomes stilled, the one Intelligence is experienced separately from the world-appearance;] just as a mixture of wine and barley-meal separates when it is not stirred. [The impulses of the mind must be stilled,] though it is difficult to fight against impulse. [The impulses of desire arise, but] whatever the mind wishes, it purchases at the expense of the soul. [Such desires feed on pride and arrogance, and] it is a greater task to quench one's own arrogance than it is to quench a raging fire. Pride is the greatest hindrance to the progress of the soul. Moderation is the greatest virtue, and wisdom is to speak the truth and to act in accordance with nature, while continuously attending to one's own self. [A man should see to his own character,] for a man's character is his destiny. [48]

Isn't it amazing how the mystic's vision is the same today as it was twenty-five hundred years ago! And see how relevant it is to our world today! For all these years we have accustomed ourselves to seeing this universe as a soulless mechanistic machine, even while living and moving within the living Thought of God. And today we are just as ignorant of who we are and where we are as people were in Heraclitus' time. Even now, so many years after Heraclitus, most of the conscious beings in this universe are still unaware that they exist within the Thought of God, and since they are unaware, how would they ever come to be aware of it? What would be some of the clues that might persuade them? Let us make a short list:

- An intensive examination of the nature of the constituency of the objects within this universe would reveal only an intangible "field" of energy from which concentrated particulate entities inexplicably emerged.

- These particulate entities would appear to be consciously and instantaneously interconnected even if they were separated by great distances.

- Individual "particles" would be impossible to locate precisely.

- There would be numerous unexplained instances of acausal connections between disassociated elements of the universe.

- On close examination, objects would appear to have no clearly defined boundaries, but would merge with the space-time from which they arose.

- The extent of this space-time universe would appear endless but finite.

- Time would move only forward, in a progressive direction.

- It would become apparent that this universe could not possibly have become as it is purely by chance.

- Elements of life would form themselves into systems of organization spontaneously as if they were intrinsically patterned to do so.

- There would appear to be invisible "forces" which impinged on large cosmic bodies, holding them in their otherwise unsupported positions.

- There would also appear to be intangible "forces" connected with the planetary bodies that would correspond in some mysterious way to material and psychological changes in human beings.

- It would eventually be determined that "ultimately, the entire universe has to be understood as a single undivided whole, in which analysis into separately and independently existent parts has no fundamental status."

- All things in this universe would appear to move together of one accord; indeed, assent would seem to be given throughout the universe to every falling grain.

- The existence of the various objects in this Thought-universe would appear to be wholly dependent upon the conscious awareness of the objects by the Thought-beings (since their consciousness is derived from the Consciousness of the Thinker).

- It would appear that the Thought-beings were under the influence of a delusory force that prevented them from knowing who they were and why they were here.

- Some, however, would establish effective communication with the Thinker through introspective prayer or meditation.

- Some very few would even "awake" from the Thought-universe, and know their identity with the Thinker.

All of these phenomena would be evidenced today if indeed the universe *were* a wholly integrated conscious Thought in the Mind of God.

To better understand the inner workings of this Thought, we can use the analogy of a dream. See how the drama played out within a dream contains a number of constituents: characters, events, interactions, emotional responses, etc. What, we might ask, is the causal mechanism at work between each of these? The answer is that they are interrelated simply by virtue of the fact that they are constituents of a common Whole. There is no causal relationship between the various characters and events in a dream; the only *cause* is the subconscious image-making faculty in the mind of the dreamer.

The entire dream is created of one piece, without internal causes and effects. Each constituent character or dream landscape is in an interlocking relationship with all other constituents within the dream. There may be a sequence of events occurring within the dream, the previous of which may be considered the *cause* of the subsequent; but, in fact, the *only* cause is the mind of the dreamer. The dreamer is the cause; but the dream itself contains no cause-effect relationships. Rather, all is played out as a concerted, coherent unit, without division into constituent parts. Likewise, it is important to note, the consciousness of the dream-character is, in fact, the consciousness of the dreamer—in a contracted form; and when the dream-character awakes, it is no longer the dream-character, but the one who was dreaming.

Now, apply this image to the world in which we live, and many of the perplexing phenomena we encounter become more easily understood. The appearance of both local and non-local acausal interrelationships, the source of human consciousness, and even the mysterious relationship of the planets to body and psyche becomes comprehensible. All is seen to be one integrated Thought-drama, produced in the mind of God. Most significantly, such a world-view satisfactorily explains the possibility of an individual consciousness "awaking", at least momentarily, to its true identity as the one Self and Source of the entire universe.

What, we must wonder, would be the effect on science if such a view were accepted? How would that change the way science sought the answers to their questions of how it all works? Not very much, I think—except in the realm of consciousness. I would hope that it would direct many toward an introspective rather than an extrospective orientation. It is through our minds that God becomes known; it is there we may communicate with Him, and there we may awaken to the reality of God as our true unlimited Self. As it was stated in the Upanishads:

> It is not what is thought that we should wish to know; we should know the thinker. 'He is my Self!' This one should know. 'He is my Self!' This one should know. [49]

All wisdom comes to us through Him, and it is only through a concentrated awareness of Him that we can "tune in" to that wisdom. Once we are able to recognize where we are and who we are (in truth), we shall be able to live and move in confidence and joy, and refer our every moment to His will.

THE LIFE OF A SELF-REALIZED MAN

O the life of a Self-realized man! It's much like yours, my friend;
I feel the prick of ennui and suffer the ignorance of men;
I know the annoying insistence of passions and the trickery of the brain;
I endure the deterioration of the body and its attendant pains,

And the requirements of providing bread for my table and a shelter for my head.

Like you, I muddle through from day to day, and find a welcome refuge in my bed.

I watch with hope the troubled world, and see no end to pain.

But, O my friends, I've shared eternity with God;

I've seen the infinite, eternal Self of all beyond this bubble of a world;

And deep down know a peace and joy unsullied by this maudlin scene.

I merged into the heart of God and saw the universe explode in form,

And then implode again, a breath-like cycle, endlessly repeated.

I balanced, poised in unblinking vision, in His still domain, at one with Him;

And saw no separation or division, nor I or Thou, nor now or then.

The pairs of opposites were no more, but cancelled out

In breathless heights of all-inclusive oneness;

And I knew the everlasting Self of God as I, the only I who ever was.

Though bound, like you, to worldly life, I'm free; my heart is calm and certain.

I know the "I" beyond my role here in this paltry play;

And when I exit from the stage, I'll still be I, backstage,

The One who plays all roles, who lives to ply His art once more

With plots, and lines, and costumes ever new.

And, even now, while taking in the very air you breathe,

And walking on the very shores of time you walk,

I breathe as well the light eternal and walk the hallowed skies.

My heart imbibes the sweetest joy time's shadows can't obscure;
And, like a man with either foot astride a threshold, I'm here,
though I am there.
I walk the world on tiptoe, with my head above the clouds;
My eyes are fixed undeviatingly on God's perpetual smile. And,
though you see me here with you, performing on the boards,
I'm there, in God's unbounded bliss, my own eternal Self.

12

TOWARD A SYNTHESIS OF SCIENCE AND GNOSIS

The scientist is possessed by a sense of universal causation ... His religious feeling takes the form of a rapturous amazement at the harmony of natural law, which reveals an intelligence of such superiority that compared with it, the systematic thinking and acting of human beings is an utterly insignificant reflection... It is beyond question closely akin to that which has possessed the religious geniuses of all ages. [50]

–Albert Einstein

Any attempt to formulate a Grand Unified Theory that leaves out the Source of all physical manifestation will result in an incomplete Theory. It seems to me that what is needed is a mergence of science with gnosis; i.e., a rethinking of the present one-sided and limited perspective on reality to include both scientific and gnostic perspectives. Such a new approach might be termed *gnoscience*. But how does the mystic convince the scientist of the truth of his vision. He can't. Mystical knowledge must be convincing on its own. If the scientist cannot accept it, he rejects it; and, well then, the worse for science. Let me draw an analogy to illustrate the difficulty involved:

Imagine that a man named John lives with his handicapped brother, Tom, in an isolated tract on the plains of Kansas. They have no access to phones, TV or movies. Imagine further that John takes a trip to New York City, spending a week or so taking in the sights. Upon John's return, he recounts to his invalid brother Tom what he saw, describing the towering skyscrapers, the subways, the culturally diverse population. Aside from a faith in his brother's honesty, how does Tom know that what John described actually exists? The answer is, 'He doesn't'. Tom cannot travel, and so he has no access to the experience his brother reports; unless and until he sees it for himself, it remains for Tom a matter of faith, or belief, maybe even conviction. But knowledge? No.

Suppose Tom stubbornly refuses to believe that what his brother reported was really true. How would John be able to prove to his brother beyond a doubt that New York really was as he described it. The answer is, 'he couldn't'. The predicament of John is similar to the predicament of one who has seen in mystical vision the transcendent Source of all existence. He can tell of it, but he can't prove it. The only way another might obtain knowledge of it is to see it for himself in a similar state of consciousness. Others, lacking that experience, might well reject the mystic's report, since it involves a means of knowledge whose existence they cannot confirm, or do not acknowledge.

Socrates tells a similar story in Plato's 'Analogy of the Cave', occurring in the *Republic*. The man who finds his way from the cave, out into the sunlight, returns to tell the others remaining in the cave about the wider reality of light which he discovered; and the others, insulted by his seemingly preposterous story, beat and kill him. Socrates went on to illustrate the meaning of that story in his own life and death. For the mystic, the question remains 'How convince others that such a transcendent vision is possible?' 'How convince those doubtful of the truth and relevance of one's experience in that exclusive environment of consciousness that what was seen is true?'

The history of mysticism is replete with accounts of the men and women who have attained that vision and who were persecuted and rejected by the people when they reported their observations of that transcendent realm. But the accumulation over a great length of time of identical reports must surely cause some effect on the doubtfulness of the empirical public! (On this subject, I would like to strongly urge those with an interest in learning more about the great mystics and their message to see my *History of Mysticism*: The *Unchanging Testament*. For more on the mystical experience itself, see my book, *The Supreme Self: The Way to Enlightenment*.) Surely, after so many have obtained that same vision, the people and the scientists will begin to rethink their rejection of the possibility of such vision and the relevance to their own worldview of the data accumulated.

It is time, I think, to acknowledge that the experience of the mystic offers a new and more profound hypothetical framework for an authentic and consistent worldview than our customarily materialistic one. It is time to open our eyes to the fact that there is a means of knowledge possessed by the few which promises a glimpse into the truth of ourselves and our universe, if only we are able to listen and to incorporate into our view of reality what those few visionaries have to say.

The question arises of whether an acceptance of gnosis such as I am advocating will necessitate merely another "faith" in theories unverifiable. The answer is "Yes, to some extent, until such theories are verified by experience." Such is the manner of all hypotheses.

But this one already has the stamp of validation, as it has been found to be true by countless experimenters. The acceptance of gnosis should result in the attempt by many others to verify it by personal experiment, just as scientists are accustomed to do. The experiment to prove to one's own certain satisfaction that God, the universal Self, exists and creates this universe is to prepare oneself to give all one's heart and mind to the endeavor to know Him – not by the scientific method (as such knowledge is precluded from science), but by the gnostic method – through prayer and contemplation.

Isn't this what has been taught by all the saints and "saviors" who've ever lived? And I would add that one should take a solemn vow not to venture an intractable opinion on the matter or write another book until one had discovered Him, and verified the truth for oneself. This was the method of the Buddha, Jesus, and other rightfully revered attainers of mystical vision. It is so rarely attained because, unlike science, which can be practiced in the midst of an academic or laboratory career, gnosis requires a period of solitary introspective contemplation in which to examine and eradicate the vestiges of ego in oneself.

As Plotinus suggested:

Withdraw into yourself and look. And if you do not find yourself beautiful yet, act as does the creator of a statue that is to be made beautiful; he cuts away here, he smoothes there, he makes this line lighter, this other purer, until a lovely face has grown upon his work. So do you also; cut away all that is excessive, straighten all that is crooked, bring light to all that is in shadow; labor to make all one glow of beauty and never cease chiseling your statue until there shall shine out on you from it the godlike splendor of virtue, until you shall see the perfect goodness established in the stainless shrine. [51]

We dare not keep ourselves set towards the images of sense, or towards the merely vegetative, intent upon the gratifications of eating and procreation; our life must be pointed towards the divine Mind, toward God.[52]

...Once There, [the soul] will trade for This nothing the universe holds – no, not the entire heavens; for there is nothing higher than This, nothing more holy; above This there is nowhere to go. All else, however lofty, lies on the downward path; she knows that This was the object of her quest, that there is nothing higher. [53]

...Without that vision, the soul is unillumined; but illumined thereby, it has attained what it sought. And this is the true Goal set before the soul: to receive that light, to see the Supreme by the Supreme; ... for That by which the illumination comes is That which is to be seen, just as we do not see the Sun by any other light than its own.

How is this to be accomplished?

Let all else go! [54]

PLATO'S CAVE

I lay in chains like all the rest, but even in my youth
I sought a way beyond this gloomy labyrinthine cave.
I'd heard the legends of a land of light, and one day
Broke my chains and began my search, exploring paths
Both dark and narrow where very few had gone before.

Alone, I felt my way through winding passageways,
Leading always upwards toward a dim but beckoning light;
And at last broke free, all unexpectedly bathed in light.
For suddenly, as though lifted on a wind divine,
I was elevated to a heavenly plane
Where I was not the man I'd been before.
The life I'd known beneath the surface,
Where only darkness reigned, was but a distant memory;
As now I beheld a glorious radiance of white engulfing me
And into which I blent.

No flickering fires, no shadowed walls, nor separate
Dancing figures differentiated here; for all was
One free vastness irradiated from above
And bright with clarity so intense I saw for miles
An endless horizon spreading everywhere at once.

In breathless awe I took it in, marveling at the breadth
And scope of this unexpected land to which I'd come,
And breathed the light-filled air so sweet and pure.

There, the very earth was mine and all the starry heavens;
And I was at the center, still, containing all.
I had become the one great light,
Begetting and illuminating every thing and beast;
There was no other to behold, as all combined in me.

And all was perfect everywhere,
Moving toward its perfect end.

No trace of self remained, but only this one eternal Beauty
I beheld shining endlessly in all.

How expansive was the freedom that I felt!
How flawless my delight!
I saw with intimate clarity Eternity's joy-filled peace,
And witnessed the breath-like ebb and flow
Of cosmic birth and death.
For, somehow, I was made to see that all revolved in me;
That I was part and whole, and yet was much, much more:
The still, unchanging eye unbound by time
That watched while time unfurled its transient array.

How long I stood there I cannot know;
Lost in vision's trance, I clung with all my power
To the tenuous gift of sight.
But thoughts rushed back to pull me down,
And I descended from the whiteness into dark once more.
My mind descended once again to self and those I'd left
Still struggling in the darkened cave,
Still unimagining what bright place lay just above.

I vowed to tell them all what place I'd found and how
They too might rise above their dungeon-life below.
That such a place existed was still unknown to all;
That life held so much more of joy and light
And endless vision none had dared to dream.
And soon I found myself returned to the world I'd known,
Below, unlit, where only artificial shadows produced the show.

And yet, sustained within my mind was what I'd seen above;
And it was this which fired my blood
And brought to these familiar scenes illumination
From my memory's so newly acquired delight.

And as I went among the dreary folk,
My eyes still brightened by the light I'd found,
I told them of my discovered land, and of the brightness there,
And how I'd made my way by following the upward trail.

But none believed me. I was an embarrassment
To friends and family who thought I'd lost my mind.
"That's very interesting", they said; "And now it's time for lunch".
While others said, "Everyone has their own ideas, you know;
I have my own beliefs as well."
And so I learned to keep my knowledge to myself, and spend
My quiet hours alone, remembering where I'd been.

And even now, my heart is drawn there still!
My eyes, still filled with vision of the light I'd seen,
Were unaccustomed now to dark;
And though I tried to focus on the customary tasks
Incumbent on the dwellers here below,
I could not wholly give myself to thoughts
And purposes of men enslaved,
Nor take delight in shadows playing on the walls.
My briefly tasted freedom rendered me unfit
For chains and games that others loved;
My heart was up above.

And so they ask, "What benefit did you derive from your escape?
You journeyed there, or so you say,
And what have you gained but blindness and disdain
For what all men hold dear?"
I have no answer to these taunts.
I only know that I have gone
Where I was meant to go, and saw a world
More real, more glorious than this shadowed one below.
I've known the joyful promise which my soul desired;
I reached the goal, the source of joy and light.
And, though I'm here among the rest, I stand there still,
Immersed in light, delighting in the far-flung landscape that I saw.
For in my heart my home is there;
I'll live there evermore.

EPILOGUE

Just to add to the interesting synchronicity relating to the writing of this current book and the concurrent publication of Richard Tarnas' ground breaking work, allow me to share some astounding astrological synchronistic correlations in my own life and work: It was on November 18, 1966 that the mystical experience came to me that utterly changed my life and put me on the path to teaching the mystical point of view. As I pointed out in my book, *The Supreme Self*, there were, at the same time as that experience, some remarkable astronomical corollaries in the heavens. There was, of course, the appearance of several major transiting aspects to my natal chart, involving the outer planets: Uranus and Pluto were conjunct at the time, along with Mars; all were closely trine to Saturn in the heavens, and conjoining my natal Neptune. The transiting Sun, Mercury, Venus and Neptune were also conjunct, and trine Saturn, forming a close sextile to the Uranus-Pluto-Mars stellium. All of this was quite singular; but most striking of all were the "progressions" occurring at the same time.

Progressions—more specifically, Solar arc progressions—are not actual occurrences in the heavens; but rather abstractions, calculated from where the specific planet or body specified once was. They show the position of the Sun, for example, where it was only days after one's birth. Taking that Sun's position when it reached a conjunction with another planet, and using the formula of one day of actual movement to represent a year's movement, it is said to be "progressed" to that planetary conjunction in that number of years. In other words, using the formula of one day for one year, the progressed position of the Sun at 28 days after my birth was said to represent the 28th year of my life. There is another milestone at the 28-29 year mark: the "Saturn return": it is when Saturn, in its normal transiting of the zodiac, returns to its original position at birth. It is said to be the time when a young person matures, and begins or settles into his or her destined career.

Saturn was nearing its "return" at the time of my mystical experience; and the Sun had "progressed" to an exact conjunction with the natal position of Neptune in my chart. Not only that; the Moon had progressed to an exact conjunction with my natal Saturn. These, one has to admit, are remarkable "coincidences". Now, let's go forward a bit: when I went to India for the second time, in May of 1978, to take initiation into *sannyas* (monkhood), the Moon had progressed to a conjunction with my natal Venus, and transiting Saturn was conjunct my natal Sun position. Incidentally, the progressed Moon was *exactly* conjunct my natal Venus on November 18, 1978 – exactly 12 years after the day of my mystical experience, when I was beginning my first teaching assignment in New York. In 1966, shortly after my mystical experience, I had vowed to become a swami in twelve years.

When the Sun progressed to Venus, the next counterclockwise natal planet after Neptune in my chart, I published *The Supreme Self* for the first time, and wrote *Jnaneshvar*, and was working on *History of Mysticism*. In time, all of my books were published, and I founded a religious organization in which to teach the philosophy of Self-realization. But by 2006, I had long retired from teaching and writing, and anticipated no further writing projects. In the few weeks surrounding March 28, 2006, however, this present book was written in a sudden unexpected outburst of creativity and enhanced awareness; twenty-eight years had passed, and *the Moon had once again progressed to a conjunction with my natal Venus.*

One can much more easily accept the synchronous correlation of life-altering experiences with the aspects between transiting planetary positions and one's natal planetary positions than one can accept or account for progressed aspects, since, after all, they are only conceptual formulas for positions, and not real positions of the planets. Nonetheless, there you are; they have a real correlation with the events and changing psychological perspectives occurring throughout one's life. The question that continually arises is "how do these various planetary 'influences' work? What is the means whereby the physical relationships between planetary bodies corresponds to the timing of psychic events in an individual?" Even though we acknowledge that the relationship between planetary positions and human psychological and physical occurrences is an acausal one, being merely synchronous and signatory, still we wish to understand the means or "mechanism" of that relationship.

It seems to me, however, that such questions are merely a product or remnant of our long-accustomed "mechanistic" view of the universe, which demands a mechanical "force" or medium through which such relationships operate. The truth is that the universe is not a great clock, but rather a great conscious Thought (*epinoia, logos*) in the Mind of God. This is what the mystics, the true seers of reality, have taught us throughout the ages. All the mystics who ever lived have stated that God is an eternal Consciousness who projects this manifested phenomenon we call "the universe" as a kind of Thought-construct; and that His Consciousness informs, animates, and lives within this projected universe and as the consciousness of individual beings. That one Consciousness permeates all animate and inanimate being. Science is on the verge of discovering this truth.

It may be that science will in time discover the method of the transmission of planetary "influences" to the physical and mental receptors on earth, but we must remember that, to put it in Bohmian terms, such explicate influences have their source in the implicate order and ultimately in the "holomovement" underlying these two levels of universal order. In other words, such influences are ultimately constituents of the Whole of the Divine design, and must be seen as originating in the one Consciousness, the Divine Mind.

The view of the universe as a Thought-construct offers a clarified vision of Bohm's concept of an underlying implicate order; implicit in such a vision is the existence of non-local relationships and the acausal interconnectedness of disparate elements within the whole Thought-fabric. The various forces—gravitational, electromagnetic, the weak and the strong—may also be seen as implicit elements of the Thought-matrix, representing the tendency toward integral cohesiveness in the structure of various wholistic systems within the larger Whole. Other phenomena, such as the discontinuous energy levels of quanta, their wave-particle duality, and the phenomena associated with relativity theory, must also be seen as potentially capable of explanation as implicit elements in the nature of God's manifested Thought. These, I feel confident, are matters which the genius of science will manage to integrate into a consistent and comprehensive Theory of Everything in the course of time.

But the most important and significant aspect of this vision of the world is that it explains how we can "tap into" and derive intelligent inspiration from that conscious Thought, and can even ascend in consciousness to the Source of that Thought. It would seem that the existence of favorable planetary energies contributes in some way in facilitating conscious access to the subtler realms of this Thought, to the ideas present in what Bohm calls "the implicate order", and even beyond the Thought to the Thinker, or "holomovement".

The fundamental fact that we must know is that this universe, and all that exists within it, including the appearance of time, is a *projection* of the one Consciousness. We can call it *maya, shakti, prakriti, epinoia, logos, thought*, or whatever other name we wish to use. It is God's projection, or emanation, and it is produced in a manner similar to our own production of dreams or mind-born imaginations. It is of the nature of Thought. And because that Thought is in the one Consciousness (God), it is constituted of God; He is therefore the Ground and Identity of all that is. This is not only the most fundamental of facts, it is the most significantly relevant to us—since it tells us who we are and what this world is in which we find ourselves. It also reveals to us the source of our joy; for God Himself is eternal Bliss, and the contemplation of God enables us also to experience that Bliss.

If only each soul could become aware of its true nature in God, and if all gave their hearts and minds to Him, this world would be a paradise of love and joy. Yet, in our world today, few turn their minds and hearts to God; and universal love for all beings as manifestations of God is rarely seen. It is therefore an unhappy and loveless world in which we now live. I sorrow for this misguided world and its mistaken views. Each day we hear of mass killings and fighting between ideational factions in all parts of the world. Cruelty and hatred are rampant. This will continue until true knowledge and adoration of the Source of our being arises in the hearts of men and women. And that can only happen one person at a time.

But let us not forget that we are yet young in the evolution of God's Thought-world. Our minds and our understanding are still evolving and expanding. We are still fallible, unsure; still subject to error. We are still capable of making unwise choices, which result in the appropriate consequences. But there are also opportunities for the evolution of understanding and the realignment of the "soul" with the governing law of love. Through every age He has led us, awakening us to greater self-knowledge and wisdom. And He will continue to lead us, to guide us, toward our perfection in Him. He has set the planets into the heavens as helpful signposts that serve to guide us unerringly on our way.

NOTES

1. Capra, Fritjof, 1975

2. Townes, Charles, in Margenau and Varghese, 1993; p. 123.

3. Nicholas of Cusa, in Beck, 1969; p. 64.

4. Nicholas of Cusa, in Dolan, 1962; pp. 105-106.

5. Ferris, Timothy, 1997; pp. 246-248.

6. Planck, Max,

7. Bohr, Neils, in Amaldi, 1966; p. 110.

8. Hoffman, Banesh, 1959; p. 179.

9. Bohm, David; quoted in Friedman, Norman, 1994; p. 95.

10. Bohm, David and Hiley, Basil, 1975; pp. 96, 102.

11. Lazlo, Ervin, in Combs and Holland, 1996; Foreword To The Second Edition, p. xiii.

12. Bohm, David, 1980.

13. Tarnas, Richard, 2006; p. 68.

14. Ibid., p. 468.

15. Ibid., P. 489.

16. Davies, Paul, 1984; p. 221.

17. Jnaneshvar, in Abhayananda, 1989; p. 237.

18. Wheeler, John, in Zurek, 1990; p. 18.

19. Simon Magus, in Roberts and Donaldson, Vol. VI, 1892; pp. 208-210.

20. Friedman, Herbert, 1990; p. 26.

21. *Svetasvatara Upanishad*, V.3.

22. *Maitri Upanishad*, 6.17.

23. *Bhagavad Gita*, Chapters VIII.17-20

24. Ibid., Chapter IX, 7-10.

25. Lao Tze, *Tao Teh Ching*, 16.

26. Chuang Tze, Chapter 22.

27. Chuang Tze, Chapter 8.

28. Ibid., Chapter 23.

29. Ibid., Chapter 6.

30. Heraclitus, fragment 88.

31. Heraclitus, fragment 30.

32. Plotinus, from Vaughan, Robert Alfred

33. Bohm, David, in Nichols, Lee, 2003; p. 105.

34. Shankara, in Prabhavananda and Isherwood, 1947; pp. 52-53.

35. Ibid., p. 64.

36. Ibid., pp. 69-70.

37. Ibid., pp. 49-52.

38. Ibid., pp. 71-72.

39. Carter Phipps, 2006; pp. 88-89.

40. Plotinus, *Enneads*, IV: 3.2: Problems of the Soul (1)

41. Ibid., IV: 3.3-4.

42. Ibid., III: 22.

43. Abhayananda, Swami, 2005; pp. 131-132.

44. Ibid., pp. 133-134.

45. Shankara, in Prabhavananda and Isherwood, 1947; p. 58.

46. Ibid., p. 118.

47. Jeans, James, *The Mysterious Universe*.

48. Heraclitus, from Abhayananda, 2002; pp. 91-93; originally adapted from fragments found in Freeman, 1962; pp. 24-34.

49. *Kaushitaki Upanishad,* III.8; based on Mascaro, 1965.

50. Albert Einstein, 1934

51. Plotinus, *Enneads*, I: 9.

52. Ibid., 15: 3.2

53. Ibid., 38: 6.34.

54. Ibid., 49: 5.7.

BIBLIOGRAPHY

Abhayananda, Swami, from *Changadev Pasashti*, in *Jnaneshvar: The Life And Works of The Celebrated Thirteenth Century Indian Mystic-Poet*, Olympia, Wash., Atma Books, 1989.

— *The Supreme Self: The Way To Enlightenment*, Winchester, U.K., O Books, 2005.

— *History of Mysticism: The Unchanging Testament*, London, Watkins Publishing, 2002.

Amaldi, Ginestra, *The Nature of Matter*, Chicago, University of Chicago Press, 1966.

Beck, Lewis W., *Early German Philosophy*, Cambridge, Mass., Belknap Press of Harvard University Press, 1969.

Bohm, David, *Wholeness And Implicate Order*, London, Routledge, 1980.

Bohm, David and Hiley, Basil, "On The Intuitive Understanding of Non-Locality as Implied By Quantum Theory", London, Foundations of Physics journal, Vol. V, 1975.

Capra, Fritjof, *The Tao of Physics*, Boulder, Shambhala, 1975.

Combs, Allan and Holland, Mark, *Synchronicity: Science, Myth, And The Trickster*, New York, Marlowe & Co., 1996.

Davies, Paul, *Superforce: The Search for a Grand Unified Theory of Nature,* New York, Simon & Schuster, 1984.

Dolan, John P. (ed.), *Unity And Reform: Selected Writings of Nicholas de Cusa*, Notre Dame, University of Notre Dame Press, 1962.

Einstein, Albert, "The Religious Spirit of Science", in Mein Weltbild, Vol. 18; 1934. Reprinted in Ideas And Opinions, p. 40.

Ferris, Timothy, *The Whole Shebang*, New York, Simon & Schuster, 1997.

Freeman, Kathleen, *Ancilla To The Pre-Socratic Philosophers,* Cambridge, Harvard University Press, 1962.

Friedman, Herbert, *The Astronomer's Universe: Stars, Galaxies, and Cosmos*, New York, W.W. Norton, 1990.

Friedman, Norman, *Bridging Science And Spirit,* St. Louis, Missouri, Living Lake Books, 1994.

Hippolytus of Rome, *Refutatio Omnium Heresium*, VI.8, in Roberts and Donaldson, 1892.

Hoffman, Banesh, *The Strange Story of The Quanta,* New York, Dover Publications, 1959.

Jeans, James, *The Mysterious Universe.*

Margenau, Henry and Varghese, Roy A. (ed.), *Cosmos, Bios, Theos*, LaSalle, Ill., Open Court, 1993.

Mascaro, Juan, *The Upanishads,* Middlesex, Penguin Books, 1965.

Nichols, Lee, (ed.), *The Essential David Bohm*, London, Routledge, 2003.

Phipps, Carter, "Death, Rebirth & Everything In Between", *What Is Enlightenment?* Magazine, Issue 32, March- May 2006.

Planck, Max, *Where Is Science Going?*

Prabhavananda, Swami and Isherwood, Christopher, *Shankara's Crest- Jewel of Discrimination*, Hollywood, Calif., Vedanta Press, 1947, 1975.

Roberts, Rev. A. and Donaldson, J. (eds.), *The Ante-Nicene Christian Library*, Edinburgh, T. & T. Clark, 1892.

Simon Magus, *Apophasis Megale*, "The GreatExposition", quoted by Hippolytus of Rome, in Roberts & Donaldson, 1892.

Tarnas, Richard, *Cosmos And Psyche*, New York, Viking, 2006.

Wheeler, John, "Information, Physics, Quantum: The Search For Links", in Zurek, Wojcieh, 1990.

Zurek, Wojcieh H., (ed*.), Complexity, Entropy, and the Physics of Information*, Reading, Mass., Addison-Wesley, 1990.

Einstein, "science without religion — 7/17
82,89
creation & dissolution 17
absolute consciousness 91
aham brahasmi, I am Brahman 92
Isaiah 2, 45:4-7 evil
I am Brahman 103
The universe — a great thought
James Jeans 106
Man and God 93